real-life
decorating
your look, your budget

Real-Life Decorating is packed with practical advice to help do-it-yourself decorators like you create rooms that fit your lifestyle and decorating style. We put the *real* in *Real-Life Decorating* with case studies of *real* homes with *real* people who share their decorating secrets and know-how.

Regardless of your style and budget, hard-working lessons and easy-to-achieve tips help you decorate your home your way with confidence and a fresh perspective. Learn how to make decorating decisions about color, pattern, furniture arranging, small spaces, storage, and more.

contents

Better Homes and Gardens®

real-life
decorating
your look, your budget

WILEY

John Wiley & Sons, Inc.

*What Does Your Home Say About You?

take our QUIZ

1

Displayed on your walls, you have:
- ○ **A.** several framed pictures of family and friends
- ○ **B.** only one or two items
- ○ **C.** items that follow your theme (chickens, apples, cows, etc.)
- ○ **D.** original art pieces by people you know

2

Your kitchen counter is usually:
- ○ **A.** very clean—you can't stand to have even one small appliance out
- ○ **B.** cluttered—a display of old cookie jars and cookbooks
- ○ **C.** congested—full of random kitchen gadgets and a TV
- ○ **D.** covered in dirty dishes

3

What item is most prevalent in your home?
- ○ **A.** books and magazines
- ○ **B.** baskets and candles
- ○ **C.** photographs
- ○ **D.** cleaning supplies

4

One item you would bring back from a trip is
- ○ **A.** a stack of pictures
- ○ **B.** a good tan
- ○ **C.** a souvenir sweatshirt
- ○ **D.** a one-of-a-kind piece of local art

5

How many items do you have on your refrigerator?
- ○ **A.** one to three
- ○ **B.** four to seven
- ○ **C.** eight to 10
- ○ **D.** so many that you can't see the refrigerator

6

If your family invited you over for a meal, after eating, you would be found
- ○ **A.** taking a nap
- ○ **B.** drinking and talking
- ○ **C.** filling coffee cups
- ○ **D.** cleaning up

7

If you could identify one color scheme in your home, it would be
- ○ **A.** neutral—beige, white, and black
- ○ **B.** warm—reds and yellows
- ○ **C.** cool—blues and greens
- ○ **D.** too hard to identify

8

What trait do you value most in your home?
- ○ **A.** creative influence
- ○ **B.** aesthetic value and style
- ○ **C.** physical comfort
- ○ **D.** pleasing scent

9

How would you classify your home organization?
- ○ **A.** meticulous—everything is in its place
- ○ **B.** health-department hit list—what's organization?
- ○ **C.** comfortably congested
- ○ **D.** organized clutter—there's a method to the madness

10 Do you deny yourself sleep, food, and fun in order to get things done?
- ○ **A.** often
- ○ **B.** sometimes
- ○ **C.** rarely
- ○ **D.** never

11 Would you pull things out of other people's trash and think, *Hey, I can use that*?
- ○ **A.** sure
- ○ **B.** maybe
- ○ **C.** doubtful
- ○ **D.** never

12 You find people who spend a great deal of time on their homes
- ○ **A.** caring—their love of life is shown in the heart of their home
- ○ **B.** boring—there is more to life than making sure your house looks good
- ○ **C.** responsible—it shows that they like to take good care of things
- ○ **D.** interesting—you admire them and wish to be more like them

13 Do you break out in a sweat when you can't get things done at home?
- ○ **A.** always
- ○ **B.** sometimes
- ○ **C.** rarely
- ○ **D.** never

14 How embarrassed would you be if a friend stopped over unannounced and your house was a mess?
- ○ **A.** ready to die—you would be in shock and might find her rude for not phoning first
- ○ **B.** a little, but you would quickly recover because you love seeing your friends
- ○ **C.** moderately—you would act hospitable, make a lot of excuses, and find a reason to move her out fast
- ○ **D.** totally numb—you would curl up into a fetal position and suck your thumb

15 Do you fret about how others might view your place?
- ○ **A.** yes—it's what you live by
- ○ **B.** sometimes—you want them to be comfortable
- ○ **C.** rarely—you like what you like
- ○ **D.** never—why waste the energy?

16 Do you have trouble throwing things away?
- ○ **A.** often
- ○ **B.** sometimes
- ○ **C.** rarely
- ○ **D.** never

17 If you had a bit of extra money, you would
- ○ **A.** buy all new expensive bedding to impress guests
- ○ **B.** buy whatever strikes you in the first store you see
- ○ **C.** treat yourself to a small cappuccino and put the rest away in a savings account
- ○ **D.** go on a trip . . . anywhere

18 When you shop for decorative stuff for the house, it is
- ○ **A.** anything goes—if you like it, you buy it
- ○ **B.** erratic—depending on the item, you might make quick or slow decisions
- ○ **C.** hectic—you get irritated with too many choices and would rather pick from just a few selections
- ○ **D.** slow and deliberate—you search dutifully for the right thing

19 When you open your pantry doors, do all the labels face out?
- ○ **A.** often
- ○ **B.** sometimes
- ○ **C.** rarely
- ○ **D.** what?

20 Do toilet paper or paper towel rolls have to go on the holder a certain way?
- ○ **A.** absolutely
- ○ **B.** you've got to be kidding
- ○ **C.** sometimes
- ○ **D.** you don't think about it

21 Does your mood change when your surroundings are not in order?
- ○ **A.** often
- ○ **B.** sometimes
- ○ **C.** rarely
- ○ **D.** never

key

1. **A:** 1 **B:** 2 **C:** 3 **D:** 4 ___
2. **A:** 2 **B:** 1 **C:** 3 **D:** 4 ___
3. **A:** 4 **B:** 3 **C:** 1 **D:** 2 ___
4. **A:** 1 **B:** 2 **C:** 3 **D:** 4 ___
5. **A:** 2 **B:** 1 **C:** 3 **D:** 4 ___
6. **A:** 4 **B:** 1 **C:** 3 **D:** 2 ___
7. **A:** 2 **B:** 3 **C:** 1 **D:** 4 ___
8. **A:** 4 **B:** 2 **C:** 1 **D:** 3 ___
9. **A:** 2 **B:** 4 **C:** 3 **D:** 1 ___
10. **A:** 2 **B:** 4 **C:** 1 **D:** 3 ___
11. **A:** 4 **B:** 3 **C:** 1 **D:** 2 ___
12. **A:** 1 **B:** 4 **C:** 2 **D:** 3 ___
13. **A:** 2 **B:** 3 **C:** 1 **D:** 4 ___
14. **A:** 4 **B:** 1 **C:** 3 **D:** 2 ___
15. **A:** 2 **B:** 3 **C:** 1 **D:** 4 ___
16. **A:** 4 **B:** 1 **C:** 3 **D:** 2 ___
17. **A:** 2 **B:** 3 **C:** 1 **D:** 4 ___
18. **A:** 4 **B:** 3 **C:** 1 **D:** 2 ___
19. **A:** 2 **B:** 3 **C:** 1 **D:** 4 ___
20. **A:** 2 **B:** 3 **C:** 1 **D:** 4 ___
21. **A:** 2 **B:** 3 **C:** 1 **D:** 4 ___

your total: ____

★ Turn the page to get your results!

37–52 points

per.fectionist impresser

You aim to impress, maybe even to wow. Everything has a place, and everything is clean and sanitized, from the countertops to the dog. Your house has a specific look, and everything in it was purposefully chosen to coordinate. Outwardly, you appear comfortable with visitors and might even entertain often. Yet inside you are nervous and often insecure about how others might view you and your home. You desire order and are willing to put aside other life demands to tend to your home. You may prefer modern touches to traditional or classic. Your home often shines with chrome or glass pieces. Colors tend to run in muted neutrals and earth tones with small splashes of quiet color. Your choice of pattern is subtle and understated, likely solid tones with a few small stripes and prints.

21–36 points

hopeless romantic

You cry during Hallmark commercials and have seen *Sleepless in Seattle* at least a hundred times. Friends tease you for your soft nature (but secretly love you for it). You want to make your house a home—a place to relax and get away from it all. Because you are so rich in sentiment, you tend to value everything in your home and find it hard to select favorites, so you don't. Thus, your house might be overloaded with photographs, artwork, and knickknacks. When shopping for new decorative items, you select with your heart first, responding to what makes you feel good rather than something that perfectly coordinates. In your house, colors tend to run to the blues and yellows with a heavy mix of patterns and textures.

69–84 points

eclectic hoarder

You are a three-dimensional thinker who probably has talents in the arts. People sometimes love or hate your ideas, but you're often told, "I would never have thought of that." You love to mix and match and throw things together just to see what happens. On the other hand, you also tend to be a closet hoarder who has trouble throwing anything away in fear that you or someone somewhere might be able to use it. In your frantic moments, you may secretly desire to toss in a match and start over. Your organizational style is erratic at best. You tend to stack items and prefer to leave most things out just in case you need them. You live by the credo that clutter is a sign of genius. There is no color or pattern tendency to speak of in your home because stuff is constantly being added.

53–68 points

comfort classic

You think your home should be a unique reflection of you; you don't mask any decorating eccentricities, you embrace them. You can't help but add to your collections—especially items such as themed vintage dishware, 1940s fruit-pattern textiles, or old store signage (hey, kitsch can be *way* cool, and there is nothing wrong with grouping it by categories). Warmth and comfort are your primary motivators when you buy pieces for the house; you want guests to feel cozy when they visit. You pay particular attention to details such as smell and color when decorating your home, so everything is a comfortable experience. You might frequent crafts shows and probably prefer homemade gifts to store-bought ones. The amount of energy you expend on blending the colors and patterns in your home is great. You tend to migrate toward reds and greens and are not afraid of vibrant prints.

chapter
ONE

{ DECORATING BASICS

- **CASE STUDY:**
  Creating Character

- **What's Wrong, What's Right:**
  Family Room

- **What's Wrong, What's Right:**
  Bedroom

- **What's Wrong, What's Right:**
  Living Room

- **Making Arrangements**

creating character

To dress her family's bland 1950s house with cottage character, Kim Majka took the saw into her own hands. By tackling small portions of the house at a time, she steadily gained the confidence and skill to add crown molding, paneled effects, and wainscoting to every room. It was painstaking work that often involved mistakes, but the enhanced features give the home the architectural character Kim craved.

living color
Kim used crisp white paint to help new built-ins and millwork stand out from taupe walls.

SAVINGS SLEUTH
Kim paired red chairs picked up at a garage sale with a farm table she and husband Matt bought at a department store sale before they had children.

light woods
Maple furniture and light oak floors create a cottage look. Plus, the two tones blend easily with other finishes.

Kim Majka pores through home furnishings catalogs, but rarely does she look at the merchandise. She studies the sets.

There's a simple explanation: Kim is addicted to molding. There is no 12-step program to help her cope—and, frankly, Kim's not interested in reforming. She keeps her miter saw well oiled and handy because she never knows when she might need to add a bit more trim to a cabinet or fit some beaded board to a wall.

When Kim and her husband, Matt, moved into their postwar Colonial-style house nine years ago, it had bare walls and "real skinny ranch molding," Kim says. "That was a big challenge to me. I feel like you can't have enough molding in a house." But with a toddler and a baby on the way, there was little room in the family budget for expensive finish carpentry. "So one Christmas, I asked for a miter saw," Kim says. "I would cut trim in the garage while my kids were napping. It's very time-consuming. I totally get why it's so costly."

The house has evolved to take on the casual cottage style Kim prefers. She beefed up molding, added wainscoting in every room, and coated all the woodwork with cheerful white paint. As she gained confidence, she tackled more ambitious projects: turning a closet in her son's room into a seating nook and re-dressing the dining room fireplace to make it look less formal. When the Majkas recently gave their kitchen a makeover, Kim designed the buffet cabinet, the homework area, and the decorative brackets that hide plumbing pipes. Artisans did the bulk of the work, but Kim visited their workshop, adding hardware and staining the pieces.

"I get crabby when I don't have a project," Kim says. "I need to be creative." This energy has fueled a side business helping other people decorate and accessorize their houses. But most of her focus remains on her own house, which she considers a work in progress. "Every year, we have a project." Kim says. "I have a lot of patience. I get a lot of satisfaction out of doing things myself. So until I have time to do it myself, I'll wait."

This year, the Majkas will start working on the family room, which doesn't have nearly enough architectural character to suit Kim. Her vision includes built-ins, a coffered and beamed ceiling, half-walls to divide the space, columns—and, of course, more molding. "It's going to be darling when we're done," she says.

Reality Check: Kitchen
Make room to grow
Expanding the square footage of the kitchen would have dramatically increased remodeling costs, so Kim Majka created openness by eliminating upper cabinets and a wall separating the kitchen from the old dining room—now a homework station.

KID
SMART

self-storage
Sam and Nick each
have file drawers
in the study area
to organize school
projects and papers.

❶ BETTER VIEWS
With a more open
kitchen, Kim supervises
homework from the
stove and backyard
play from the sink.

❷ BUFFET STYLE
Using magazine pictures
for inspiration, Kim
designed the buffet with
loads of hidden storage.

❸ WARM WELCOME
Kim made the window
boxes that dress the
exterior of her home.

❹ ELBOW ROOM
Dual computers and a
wall-to-wall desk give
the boys—and parents—
plenty of work space.

smart art
Kim made the botanical artwork by pressing leaves from the yard into store-bought picture frames.

Reality Check: Swap
Who says it has to be a living room? When Kim and Matt Majka found their formal living room underutilized, Kim turned it into the dining room and converted the former dining room into a convenient homework station by the kitchen.

curb appeal
When a neighbor put a dining set at the curb, Kim took the chairs, repainted them, and re-covered the seats.

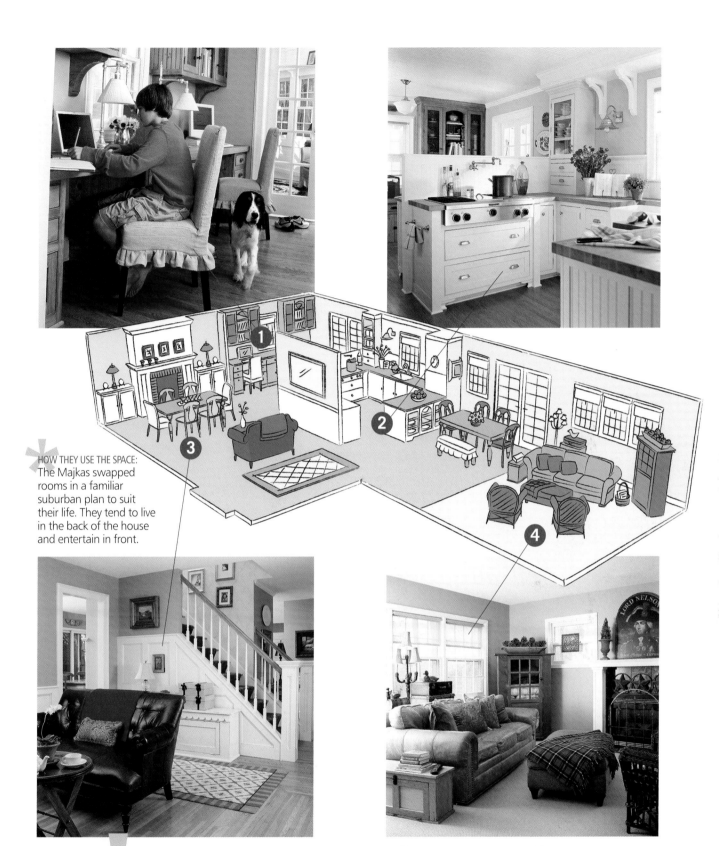

HOW THEY USE THE SPACE:
The Majkas swapped rooms in a familiar suburban plan to suit their life. They tend to live in the back of the house and entertain in front.

✳reworking a floor plan

When the Majkas moved into their home, they assigned furniture according to the prescribed floor plan. But Kim saw other possibilities. ❶ In the original dining room Kim laid out a study area with room for dual computers, files, and school projects. ❷ When remodeling the kitchen, Kim kept the same footprint but designed a half-wall between the kitchen and the study area, integrating the two rooms. ❸ Kim turned the living room into a dining room with a cozy seating area where the family can greet and entertain visitors. ❹ The family room off the kitchen is still a favorite casual gathering place.

like new
Kim painted a yard-sale chest black for a crisp new look and slipcovered a bold-pattern wing chair to accent it.

❝There's a difference between being artistic and creative. I'm creative.❞

—KIM MAJKA, homeowner

nook-keeping
Rather than eat up floor space with furniture, Kim turned an extra closet into this hangout nook.

③

Reality Check: Skills
Patience is key to success

When you are fueled by creative energy and optimism, nothing seems too big a project to take on. Kim Majka taught herself to install trim work while her two young boys took naps. While decorating the family's two-story Colonial, she added painting, refinishing, and sewing to her repertoire. Doing it herself has a learning curve, however: "If there's a mistake, it's my fault," she says. Kim learned how painstaking finish carpentry can be. The measuring, cutting, and fitting of the beaded board and crown molding in the boys' room took her a whole winter.

④

① MASTER PLAN
The master bedroom includes soothing, earthy colors, a comfortable reading chair, and a plump bed dressed with layers of natural fabrics.

② IF A TABLE FITS
Because she keeps room measurements with her when she shops, Kim knew the rustic drop-leaf table would fit this tight space in the bath.

③ IN THE DETAILS
The boys' bedroom can hold a crowd thanks to this built-in bench that's large enough to sleep on during overnights.

④ SHARED SPACE
In a shared bedroom, twice as much stuff accumulates. Kim provided display space for sports memorabilia with the plate rail and made pickup time easier with handy wall hooks. The beaded board adds cottage character.

wrong size lampshade

wrong size artwork

wrong size table

WHAT'S WRONG, WHAT'S RIGHT:
family room

AFTER CAREFUL PLANNING, you've finally created a living room with a sofa you love, a color scheme that draws you in, and accessories that tickle your fancy. Yet, like the princess who could feel the pea through a mound of mattresses, you sense something in the room just isn't quite right. What to do? Assess the scale of the elements.

Three common problem areas when rounding out a room are the scale and proportion of the tables, wall art, and lighting. Pull those into line and rest on your accomplishments.

cocktail tables:
Though we load them with decorative accessories, they have one essential function: to hold beverages within easy reach. For that reason, a table should be about two-thirds the length of a sofa so that everyone seated can comfortably reach forward to set down a drink. Plus, this proportion looks balanced.

wall art:
Pieces are commonly hung too high over a sofa—and in far too small a scale. A single vertical piece is simply too skinny. As a general rule, artwork, whether it is a rectangular piece, a pair of prints, a trio, or a grouping, should have a width between one-half and two-thirds of the sofa length and should be horizontally centered over it.

Another rule of thumb for hanging artwork is to center pieces at eye level, which is generally 5 feet up from the floor for the average adult. If the sofa is low, hang the artwork lower so it doesn't seem to float off into space. Usually, leaving 6 inches between the top of the sofa and the bottom of the art looks pleasing. But that's not a hard-and-fast rule. Adjust according to your eye.

lighting:
Choosing table lamps can be tricky. Success means not only the right lamp height but also the right scale of lampshade. Ideally, a reading lamp and its shade should direct light over your shoulder and onto your reading material. A shade emits ambient light through its drum and out the top, but also directs task light out the bottom. To do this correctly, a shade should be wider than its base and should be low enough to conceal the socket.

✔ Reality Check: Artwork
Think you can't afford "real" art?
Skip the frame. Paintings on canvas stretchers can look chic unframed. You'll save hundreds of dollars.
Buy local. **Shop local art fairs and galleries for artists of regional acclaim (and lower price tags).**
Start small. **Smaller works can cost less. Build a wall grouping over time.**
Take a photo op. **Black-and-white photography is among the most affordable. Also search photography books for images to clip and frame.**

right for the light
A wider and deeper shade covers the socket and casts light.

stronger in a pair
Two prints hung lower better suit the sofa length and the eye.

better by a long stretch
The longer table is now within reach of every seat on the sofa.

+ + = right

WHAT'S WRONG, WHAT'S RIGHT:
bedroom

wrong size nightstands

wrong size artwork

too many pillows

WHY IS THE BEDROOM THE LAST PLACE we decorate? We spend more time there than anywhere else in the house, yet it's the room we rarely tackle—maybe because it's rarely seen by anyone outside our family. But why not impress yourself and create a cozy haven in the room that can make or break your day? After all, no one says they woke up on the wrong side of the dining room. Here are three ways to fix common problems in your bedroom decor.

pillows:
We all love pillows—the squishy soft embrace, the extra support, the terrific colors. But sometimes that adoration can be a little too much infatuation and not enough reasoning. Who wants to waste precious minutes tossing pillows off the bed just to find a spot to sleep or risk being buried under an accent pillow avalanche? Instead, limit your pile to three decorative pillows, plus the standard pillows you need to sleep. You'll keep your bed tidier, and you'll eliminate one more chore before bedtime. Now that's love.

art:
Perfectly framed by a bit of crown molding above and an expanse of headboard below, the 4–5 feet of wall above the bed is well-suited for almost any display. Well, almost. Proportion is a huge challenge when picking art for such a prime piece of real estate. But don't shy away; go bold with a commanding art arrangement. This might mean one large painting or print, or a series of pieces. Or try a large wall hanging, a tapestry, a piece of stretched fabric, or a decorative paint treatment. Your bedroom is the perfect place to make a personal art statement.

nightstands:
It's unfortunate that the first furnishing we see each morning and the last one we see each night is often the most neglected piece in the house—the nightstand. A too-low or too-high nightstand keeps surfaces out of reach from the bed. And a too-small piece gets cluttered with junk. Look at your nightstand as a storage unit for the stuff that helps you get to sleep or wake up. If you are a voracious reader, get a nightstand with a shelf and drawer to hold books and magazines. The best part of choosing a nightstand is that it's so individual—you pick the piece that works best for you.

Reality Check: Night-Light
For a great alternative to the traditional space-hogging bedside lamp, try a pair of wall-mounted lamps instead.
How to choose. Trust your taste. This modern, streamlined model doesn't intrude on the serene feel of the room.
How to install. For proper reading light, install lamps so they cast light over your shoulder and onto the page while you're sitting in bed. Typical height is 24–28 inches from the bed's surface but can differ depending on how tall you are.

the big time
The large canvas fits the space better and was inspired by the throw pillow.

store more
Larger nightstands hold more stuff and are within easy reach of the bed.

simple life
A few well-chosen pillows make the bed beautiful and accessible.

+ + = right

making
arrangements

Pulling together any room can be a bit of a puzzle. But with the right pieces and placement, your spaces can be picture perfect.

WHEN AN OUTDOOR VIEW IS A ROOM'S DEFINING FEATURE, PLAN AN ARRANGEMENT THAT ALLOWS EVERYONE TO ENJOY THE SCENE.

● Face the sofa to the windows, then add chairs flanking a versatile ottoman. Pulling the grouping into the center of the room creates an intimate feeling for conversation and allows a logical traffic pattern into the seating area and through the room.

● In a larger living area, seating could expand with a longer sofa (with four seats) facing the window and at a right angle to a love seat that faces a pair of upholstered chairs.

● Keep tall accessories such as lamps from blocking the view. And if the best lamp placement is at the interior of the room, ask an electrician if an outlet can be installed in your floor to avoid lengths of cords along the floor.

accent a view
LIVING ROOM

IF YOUR MAIN LIVING AREA DOUBLES AS YOUR HOME OFFICE, HERE ARE SOME SOLUTIONS TO HELP MAKE IT WORK.

● Consider what you really need, and avoid the temptation to overcrowd.

● Divide the space into living and working zones, and anchor each with a major furniture piece. In the living area (optimally in the center of the room), start with a sofa. A chair (or two, if space allows) and coffee, console, and occasional tables fill out the scene.

● A small storage ottoman can pair with the chair or stand alone as an extra seat while containing files or other work supplies.

● Keep the workstation in a corner computer armoire so you can neatly close up shop. Such units have pullout keyboard trays, and the doors can often be adapted as bulletin boards. Add a furniture-style file cabinet for concealed storage.

LIVING ROOM
work zone

entertainment

UNLIKE THE BEHEMOTHS OF THE '80S, TODAY'S SECTIONALS ARE TRIM, SLEEK, AND A SMART ADDITION TO A LIVING ROOM.

● A sectional is a perfect supporting player in a media room. Position it for optimum viewing and eye safety (your eyes should be level with the middle of the screen, and you should be no closer to the TV than three times the diagonal measurement of its screen) as well as for access to electronics and unobstructed traffic flow.

● Keep the rest of the arrangement simple, with an angled chair (or two, depending on the size of the room and sectional).

● Utilize two storage ottomans as easy-to-reach tables and extra seating for game-day gatherings.

● A floor lamp casts a glow for reading without taking up the space of a table.

EDIT FURNITURE TO THE PIECES YOU NEED AND ARRANGE THEM FOR **HOW YOU LIVE.**

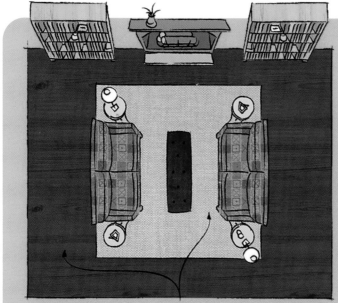

IS THE FIREPLACE (OR SOME OTHER ARCHITECTURAL FEATURE) YOUR FIXATION? OFTEN THE SIMPLEST ARRANGEMENT IS THE BEST.

● Love seats or sofas share the view when placed at right angles to the focal point.

● In a room with a fireplace and bookcases, facing seats with a long ottoman or coffee table in between instantly create a convivial conversation area with shared surfaces for books or drinks, and an unobstructed traffic flow through the room.

● Small accent and side tables allow task lighting for reading and are handy spots for drinks. In a larger living room, console tables could fit snugly behind sofas to display accessories.

focal point LIVING ROOM

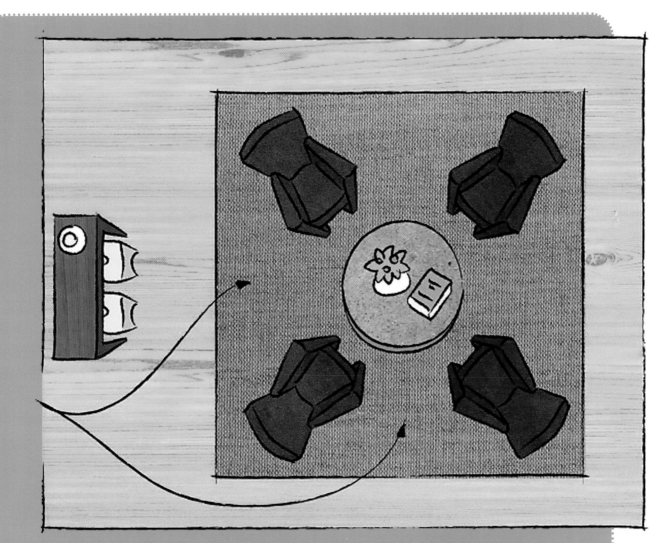

IF YOUR HOME HAS A SMALL SITTING SPACE, TAKE ADVANTAGE OF IT WITH FOUR COMFORTABLE, MATCHING ARMCHAIRS ARRANGED AROUND A COFFEE TABLE.

This plan is ideal for sharing a drink or cup of coffee while chatting after dinner—and it is as comfortable for two people to converse as it is for four. A pair of ottomans stored under a console table can be called into service as needed for footstools or extra seating.

conversation LIVING ROOM

Four perfect pieces
classic furniture that works in every living area—and beyond

①

ARMLESS CHAIRS
Angled in or out, these chairs ensure easy-to-move, stylish seating and take up less width.

②

LOVE SEAT PAIRS
Facing each other or at right angles, this team never disappoints for lounging or conversing.

③

MOVABLE OTTOMANS
Get two if you have room. Use them for seating, foot propping, a surface, or storage.

④

CONSOLE TABLES
Slip these slim wonders behind a sofa or against a wall wherever you need a surface.

play date
SPARE ROOM

IF TOYS, GAMES, AND KIDDIE CRAFTS ARE OVERTAKING YOUR LIVING SPACE, CONJURE A CREATIVE CORNER IN A SPARE ROOM.

- Push a daybed (or twin bed) lengthwise along a wall to liberate the middle of the room as a center for the arts (aka an arts and crafts table complete with kid-size chairs and benches at the height of their little bums).
- Dedicate wall and corner space to imagination stations—an easel, puppet show stand, or chalkboard.
- Include a bookcase in this TV-free zone, and make the daybed a cuddly spot for reading with squishy pillows.
- Decorate with a medium to bright color palette so kids will find it fun to hang out there.
- Keep smart surfaces in mind, too. Washable bed coverings and rugs are key. (Consider the new crop of indoor-outdoor rugs that can literally be hosed down if need be.) If you have carpet, determine your comfort level with paints and markers. If they'll be allowed, store a tarp or old sheet in the closet to use as a carpet cover-up.

RATHER THAN SPREADING CRAFTS PROJECTS OUT ON YOUR LIVING ROOM FLOOR, DEVOTE PARTS OF YOUR SPARE ROOM TO YOUR CRAFTING HOBBIES.

● Think of the bed as a table for laying out patterns, planning quilt squares, or sorting snapshots.

● Organize small supplies—and a sewing machine—in a crafter's armoire that keeps tools within easy reach yet is a snap to close up when guests arrive.

● Use dressers or bookcases with open bins to hold folded fabrics, buttons, papers, tools, and crafts magazines. Spread out small projects on their tops.

● Include a supportive armchair and a reading lamp for knitting or needlework. The chair is also a place for someone to visit with you while you work.

● Keep an iron and ironing board in the closet so you don't have to lug them across the house.

be crafty SPARE ROOM

NO ONE WANTS TO STARE AT THE STAIR-STEPPER IN YOUR LIVING ROOM, BUT IF YOU PUT IT IN THE BASEMENT, IT'LL BE OUT OF SIGHT AND OUT OF MIND. TURN A SPARE ROOM INTO A MINI GYM—WITH ENOUGH ROOM FOR A GUEST BED (AND A POST-WORKOUT NAP).

● Make it feel like a fitness center by including a treadmill, elliptical machine, or stationary bike, plus a small weight-lifting area and space to unroll a yoga mat (it stows under the bed) or do step aerobics.

● Add a TV so you can follow a workout routine or catch the news (or your DVR backlog) while you get your heart rate up. The TV is also handy when you like talk shows but your guests are reality TV fans.

● Even better? Let your guests use the treadmill as a temporary clothes rack rather than you heaping your own clothes on it every day in your bedroom!

● Scale and wall mirror? Totally up to you.

exercise daily
SPARE ROOM

SPARE ROOM
work it

A DESK STUFFED IN THE DINING ROOM ISN'T THE IDEAL HOME OFFICE. LET A MURPHY BED AND SMART TACTICS TRANSFORM A SPARE BEDROOM INTO THE ULTIMATE WORK ZONE.

- Murphy beds can be as little as 16 inches deep and look like a finished cabinet when closed. Tuck this secret sleeper between bookcases (or cabinets with lateral files) for an impressive wall of storage for books, manuals, files, and supplies.
- Use colorful magazine files and storage boxes to keep paperwork tidy and attractive on the shelves.
- Choose a desk that suits your space. A corner unit makes use of what was once "dead" space in a room, and it stays out of the way when the bed flips down.
- If space is tight, arrange an armchair and table in front of the Murphy bed, then scuttle them off to the far corner when guests arrive.

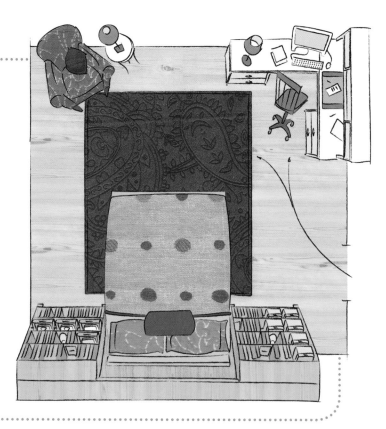

IF THE ROOM HAS A CLOSET, CONVERT IT TO **FILE STORAGE** WITH FILE CABINETS OR BINS.

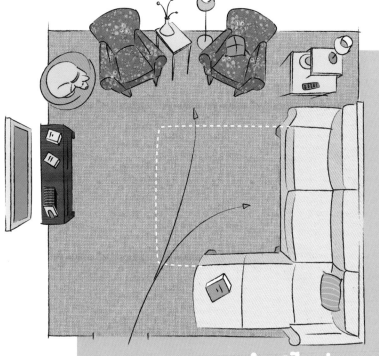

NO GUEST ROOM? NO PROBLEM. WITH A STYLISH SOFA-SLEEPER YOU CAN OFFER GUESTS A PLACE TO STAY WITHOUT COMPROMISING YOUR FAMILY ROOM'S FORM AND FUNCTION.

- A sectional offers plenty of seats for watching movies and comes with a full- or queen-size sleeper.
- No room for a sofa, much less an extra set of armchairs? Consider a pair of armchairs that flip out to single-size sleepers. Some ottoman styles also come with twin or cot-size flip-out sleepers.
- Be sure to include a small side table—it will function as a nightstand for guests.
- If you're in the market for a new TV, consider wall-mounting a flat-panel model to save valuable floor space. A low console holds components and DVDs.

overnight guests SPARE ROOM

have fun

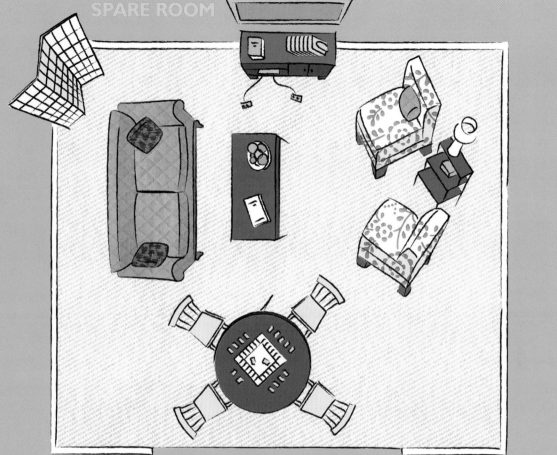

EVERY NIGHT IS GAME NIGHT WHEN YOUR SPARE ROOM HAS PLENTY OF SEATING AND PLAYING SURFACES.

● Pulling maneuverable seating into the room means more people can join the fun. It also makes room for a game table so the competition can get serious.

● The sofa and upholstered chairs are within reach of the cocktail table—and a deck of cards or a board game. The chairs scoot and twist to gain the best vantage of the TV.

● The coffee table's top lifts to reveal storage so it can serve as a playing surface, then conveniently stash board games, cards, puzzles, and video games.

● The triple-tier side table provides additional space for games—or drinks and snacks.

● A game table and chairs are perfect for poker night, complicated board games, puzzles, and extra setup space.

Room arranging

if rearranging furniture isn't cutting it, try one of these ways to rearrange your rooms—repurposing them to function for the way you live.

1

Got kids?

Kids need a place to play and keep toys and gear. If you have an eat-in kitchen, transform your dining room into a playroom.

2

Be my guest

If you've got a guest room, chances are it sits empty most of the time. Reinvent it for crafts, work, media or whatever you'll use every day.

3

Dine time

If your home lacks a formal dining room and you love to entertain, reclaim your family room as a dining space—especially if you already have a living room, too.

4

Forget being formal

Do you really live in your living room or just look at it as it takes a backseat to the family room? Make it into a home office or library or game room and live it up!

chapter
TWO

{ COLOR & PATTERN

- **CASE STUDY:**
  Decorating by Leaps and Bounds

- **How to Pick a Paint Color**

- **Afraid of Wallpaper? Get Over It!**

- **How to Mix Pattern**

- **Escape from Beige Land**

Brent adheres to a philosophy he calls design empowerment—meaning, to borrow a familiar slogan, "just do it." If a room needs a splash of color, grab a few art canvases and slap some paint on them or create an abstract collage from colorful paper. Frame it, and it's original artwork. "It's quicker, more effective, and it's a great creative outlet," Brent says.

His philosophy applies to hanging artwork (chances are the arrangement will cover the old holes), arranging accessories (he constantly rearranges), and placing furniture (there's always room for a new piece). Do it when inspiration strikes, he believes, even if it isn't perfect. You can always go back and change it.

Design empowerment also means not being afraid to incorporate pieces at varying price points with different looks. Forget the perfection of furniture showrooms and start layering the fabulous wares you find as you come across them, whether they're from discount retailers or a high-end boutique.

In a living room reading corner, for example, Brent started with a piece of distressed tin he snatched from someone's garbage. He reupholstered a chair from his father's basement and set it beside nesting tables from Target, which hold a pricier lamp from a home interiors store. Brent shies away from buying all his furnishings at one place, opting instead for an acquired look. "It's much more interesting that way," he says.

After all, pieces and the stories behind them give a room its soul. That's why the Hodges believe in following instincts. You can always tweak, repurpose, and rearrange. But just get started now, Brent says: "It's quicker to get to something you love by just taking action and doing it."

"PEOPLE TEND TO OVERTHINK DESIGN. SOMETIMES YOU JUST NEED TO DO IT AND SEE IF IT WORKS."

— BRENT HODGE, homeowner

SHAPE UP
When accessorizing the dining room shelf, *above*, Bent assembled flat, curvy, narrow, and wide shapes. He also blends matte, shiny, and rustic finishes for textural interest. Mismatched hardback books become accents with his trick: Turn the jackets inside out.

NOD TO NOSTALGIA
The liquor cart, *above right*, is a throwback to the cocktail hour aesthetic of the 1940s and 1950s. Brent made the paint-splatter artwork.

GOOD
IDEA

FINDERS, KEEPERS The Hodges found this old plywood sign, from a nearby manufacturing plant, in their basement when they moved in. It not only pulls in the coral hue from the adjacent sunroom, but it's a great dinner conversation piece.

PLANT
OFF ...

5297 RIVER RD.
ONE BLOCK WEST
ACROSS R.R. TRACK

FLEXIBLE SEATING Megan and Brent can easily pull the bench up to the table for additional seating. The tripod lamp fills the corner with atmospheric light—and shapely impact.

Reality Check: Restoring charm

Bye-bye, froufrou. **The Hodges looked beyond the home's decor when they bought it. Behind busy wallpapers, lace doilies, and bric-a-brac, they saw built-in bookcases, beautiful moldings, original fireplace tile, and warm wood floors.** Hello, simplicity. **Rather than let the long living room amble, Brent focused on seating around the fireplace and staged the center of the room as a chic entry with a console, chandelier, and rug.**

MAKE AN ENTRANCE
The home lacked a formal foyer, so Brent created a focal point with a lamp, mirror, table, and art objects, *above*, opposite the front door.

RADIATE STYLE
Radiators can be charming. Use their ledges for display, *right*. The curtains are made from men's suiting fabric.

DIVERSE MATERIALS
Brent covered the chimney wall, *far right*, in grass cloth to introduce texture to the living room.

"I DON'T LIKE MY HOME TO FEEL DECORATED. I LIKE AN ACQUIRED LOOK—ONE THAT TELLS A STORY."

— BRENT HODGE

ROOM TO GROW
The Hodges wanted to avoid babyish pastels and create a bright, visually stimulating nursery. They chose an unthemed look so that Owen can add things he thinks are cool, such as fish or dinosaurs.

A SQUARE DEAL

To create the wall detailing, Megan and Brent painted it white, then marked off a grid with 1-inch painter's tape. They painted each block a different color, then removed the tape to reveal the 1-inch borders between squares. "It's easier to do it this way because you paint the whole wall at once. Plus, it creates a windowpane look," Brent says.

BRINGING UP BABY ON GOOD DESIGN

see well:
In Owen's changing area, *left*, a wavy mirror catches his gaze while acting as art beneath open shelves. Under the bottom shelf, Megan added a strip of low-voltage rope lights that offer dim light for diaper changes in the dark.

be mod:
Inspired by a rug motif, Brent cut mod squares from plywood, *below far left*, painted them with leftover wall paint, then hung them in overlapping layers from thin chains screwed into the ceiling. They serve as overhead art for Owen and an eye-catcher to all who enter.

add oomph:
By painting large contrasting blocks behind framed art, *left*, Brent makes small pieces look larger and visually pop from the wall.

HOW TO PICK A

paint color

Paint is the cheapest and fastest way to infuse color and personality in your home. So if you're eager to get some color on those bland walls, here's a step-by-step guide to picking the perfect paint hue for you.

bare white walls

color try-outs

COLOR CONFIDENCE

CHOOSING A PAINT COLOR IS ONE of the most challenging, mind-boggling parts of decorating. You can feel completely overwhelmed by the sheer number of choices and struggle to find just the right color to match your furnishings (which is why so many of us are stuck in neutral). But there's hope: In just three simple steps you can learn the best way to pick a paint color, and in the process, find the perfect hue for your home.

get inspired: The first step to choosing a paint color is finding your inspiration. What colors bring you joy? What shade is your all-time favorite outfit? Do you prefer the warmer seasons of summer and fall or cooler spring and winter? Color is an emotional experience as much as a visual one, so turn inward when looking for hues to line your walls. The current decor is also vital to this decision, because buying a few gallons of paint is cheaper than buying a new sofa or rug.

For color ideas that already exist in your home, look to collections, artwork, fabrics or rugs, and even garden plants for inspiration. If you're still stumped, grab a book or magazine and start tabbing pages that spark your interest.

pick a color: Next, narrow down your options. After you've homed in on your source of color inspiration, look to the color wheel for the hue that will best fit your needs.

Arranged in a pinwheel, the color wheel shows the power of contrasting and complementary colors. Primary hues red, blue, and yellow form the base of the wheel, while secondary colors orange, green, and purple (created from mixing primary colors) are next. Last in the wheel are tertiary colors (yellow-orange, red-orange, yellow-green, blue-green, red-purple, and blue-purple), which mix both secondary and primary colors.

For a color scheme with punch, opt for hues on opposite sides of the color wheel—if your color inspiration is your orange sofa, opt for green or

PICK A PAINT FINISH

type of finish	strengths of the finish	weaknesses of the finish		best place to use it
Flat	Nonreflective surface quality makes walls appear smooth and uniform (hides imperfections well).	Dull sheen makes stains, fingerprints, or grease marks difficult to remove.		Best in low-activity areas such as adults' bedrooms, dining rooms, living rooms, and ceilings.
Eggshell Satin Semi-Gloss	Sheen varies from little to lots; all provide a cleanable surface that's not too shiny.	Slightly reflective quality picks up on some wall imperfections.		Best in medium- to high-activity areas such as family rooms, bathrooms, kitchens, and kids' rooms.
Gloss	The tough, stain-resistant finish holds up to frequent scrubbing.	Highly reflective quality shows off even minor surface imperfections.		Best in high- to very-high-activity areas such as kitchens and on cabinets and doors, or wherever you want a glam look.

|> get inspired

Inspiration can come from anywhere; you just have to take a step back and notice. Perhaps the hue is hiding in the fabric of your favorite accent pillow or in your backyard flower garden. And, if the main color in an inspiration piece seems a little too dramatic, check out the accent colors as well. If you're still struggling with where to begin, grab a magazine and absorb page after page of color palettes, tearing out those that suit your fancy.

2 > pick a color

Time to pick your paint using your inspiration and the color wheel. For this story, we wanted a monochromatic scheme to match the existing orange sofa and chair. So a shade of yellow was taken from some pillow fabric and red-orange from a vase of dahlias. To ensure the color options were the same intensity as the inspiration objects, we laid paint strips in a line and picked hues in the same row (i.e., color #2015-20 is the same intensity— although a different hue—as #2016-20 and 2017-20, and so on).

3 > try it out

The plethora of paint choices is slimmed down to a select few. It's time to test the finalists in the actual room by painting swatches on the wall. Observe the effects light has on your color choices, as well as how they look with your furnishings and artwork. After observing the yellow and red-orange swatches for a couple of days, we decided that we preferred a monochromatic scheme and opted for yellow paint for the walls.

blue walls. Or, if you prefer a more harmonious scheme, choose colors next to each other on the color wheel—let your orange sofa sidle up to a yellow or red wall. On the other hand, if you are simply ga-ga for one particular color, go monochromatic using different shades and tints of the same color: Put the orange sofa against a peach wall.

Shade and tint are just as important as the color you choose. A shade is a color with black added (purple becomes plum); a tint is a color with white added (purple becomes lilac). Look at a paint strip: The shaded color is at the bottom of the strip, while the tinted hue is at the very top. As you might suspect, shades add drama and intensity to a room, while tints bring serenity. If you're worried that your color pick is too intense (or too bland), opt for a hue one or two bars up or down the paint strip.

try it out: Once you've whittled down your choices, the last step in picking a paint color is to test your final color picks in the room. This step is often skipped, but is probably the most important part of choosing a paint color.

Observing the color in its environment, even on a small scale, gives you a much clearer picture of how the hue will look than trying to imagine it from a 1-inch sample on a paint swatch. Several paint companies offer poster-size swatches, plastic paint packets, and miniature pots so consumers can try out their favorite colors without having to commit to an entire quart. The tiny tester containers cost about $5 and allow you to paint a 2 × 2-foot swatch on the wall.

Paint your final choices on the wall, then live with them for a few days. See how they look with your furnishings, and notice how they affect your mood. Pay particularly close attention to the effects of natural and artificial light on the hue. For instance, in north-facing rooms without much sun, you might find your favorite paint looks dark. In sunnier spaces, the same color might look totally washed out. As you'll see, the amount and quality of light in a room can drastically change the appearance of a paint color. If your first picks don't pan out, try the test again with your second choices. Give it time, and be patient. The perfect paint color for your walls will make itself apparent.

PAINTER'S TOOL BOX

five handy tools are all you'll need to start your next paint project

❶ Rollers and trays
Ideal for an even coat on open surfaces. Choose a low nap for smooth walls, or a high nap for walls that are textured.

❷ Trim brush
Its angled head is made for painting tricky edges—from windowpanes to trim.

❸ Brushes
Perfect for painting uneven, smaller surfaces, but make sure coats go on evenly.

❹ Painter's tape
With a range of adhesive strengths, it's ideal for creating stripes or protecting outlets.

❺ Paint pads
Built like large sponges, they help apply an even coat to hard-to-reach places.

afraid of wallpaper? get over it!

Pretty patterns in artful combinations can bring a boring living room to life. And hanging wallpaper has never been easier—we promise.

the before

SOFT AND SUBTLE
For a relaxed look

So you're scared that boldly patterned walls will throw your decor into a tailspin. Not to worry. Plenty of papers, many in soft colors and petite patterns, are designed to do exactly the opposite. The pale green-on-tan Sputnik design on the window wall, for instance, adopts a supporting role. It creates a soothing backdrop with just enough color and texture to be noticed, but with enough restraint to avoid becoming the center of attention.

IN THE MIX:
When pairing wallpapers, pay particular attention to color and scale.
1 The subtle green-on-tan coloration of this pattern helps the paper fade into the distance, making it an ideal choice for covering large areas of wall.
2 With its aubergine squares, this is a good transition paper because it combines the background color of the first paper with a more graphic and noticeable pattern.
3 As the most graphic paper in the group, this is the perfect choice for the fireplace surround—a prominent fixture that called out for something bold yet naturally simple.

color cue
Let furniture guide your wallcovering colors. This sofa inspired beige backgrounds.

GOOD
IDEA

less mess
With this
nonwoven
wallpaper, simply
prime the wall,
roll on paste, and
hang dry strips.

1

2

GO FOR BOLD
Strong color statements

If you're the adventurous type, walls in a bold, graphic print (or several of them) can look stunning. If the room has a high ceiling or lots of open floor space, larger patterns and colors can make the room feel more intimate. Start with a bold neutral on a paper with a fairly traditional pattern, such as stripes, but in a colorway, such as the blue and brown one shown here, that commands attention. Continue with a secondary paper that plays off the first. Finish with a design that's altogether different.

IN THE MIX:
Wallpapers with more advancing patterns can make a vast room (this living room has 11-foot ceilings) feel more inviting.
❶ The starting point: a casual stripe that has enough interest to pull the walls visually into the room yet not overpower the other papers.
❷ A wide stripe amps up attention on the fireplace wall.
❸ A large floral print with trailing vines and leaves in darker colorations helps turn the fireplace into a whimsical, artsy attention-getter.

HANG TIME
Installation made easy

Trying to select the right wallcovering for your project? Consider newer nonwoven wallcoverings—they're easy to hang, reusable, and strippable. If you're still not convinced, read on.

Perfect pick for first-timers
You don't need a lot of gear. Simply prime the wall and let it dry thoroughly. Next, roll paste on the wall, then hang the dry paper strips. No more messy water-dipping to activate pasted papers or brushing paste onto lengths of floppy wallcovering. You don't even need a table. Just place the roll on the floor at the baseboard, pull up the first strip, press by hand, then trim with a straight edge and a sharp blade at top and bottom. No precutting necessary. Pull up next strip and repeat.

Easy pattern and seam matching
Just eyeball it. Because you don't precut paper and you match repeat—the amount of space over which the pattern plays out before replicating itself—with the roll resting at the baseboard, pattern matching is a breeze. (Small motifs and vertical stripes are easiest for beginners.) Plus, nonwoven papers don't shrink upon drying, meaning no gaps—now or later.

Stronger paper, less tearing
Nonwoven paper strips go on dry. The chances of getting a good, clean cut during installation are greater. Plus, the more durable paper is easier to manipulate in corners without wrinkling or tearing. All this means fewer mistakes and a faster job.

Slick removal
Just peel it off—really! No more arduous stripping with scrapers and solutions. Simply lift the top corner and peel off a full strip.

RESOURCE
Still need a pro?

Search the National Guild of Professional Paperhangers' Web site (www.ngpp.org) for wallpaper installation tips or to find an installer in your area.

HOW TO
MIX
pattern

Paint may be the cheapest and fastest way to add color to your home, but pattern is the easiest way to add personality. The key is to have a little (but not too much) restraint. Here's a step-by-step guide to help.

Show the world that you're anything but pattern-shy. Paper your foyer with an eye-catching print, then continue the look by adding panels made from a contrasting pattern to the back of the front door and a rug on the floor.

LESSON FOUR
it's ok to mix plaids and florals

Not to worry if you're the type who's passionate about plaids but also fond of floral prints. As the Brits have known for centuries, you can have beautiful bunches of roses on your walls and bold buffalo checks on your windows. To make the juxtaposition work, you simply have to select patterns that share a common color. Here, for example, the pink and green checks relate to the pink and green flowers found in the wallpaper and on the upholstery.

5

LESSON FIVE
coordination is key

Contrary to what you may have learned in elementary school, patterns don't have to match, even in the same room; they simply have to coordinate. You can pair a wild tropical fruit print with a modified Asian motif of lotus flowers and goldfish as shown here. You can do this because both prints share a common color palette of yellows, oranges, blues, and greens. The same applies to the other patterns in this picture—they all share colors found in the wallpaper.

LESSON SIX
size matters (so does scale)

6

Artfully shaped objects can be enhanced with pattern. The trick? Pay particular attention to size and scale. For example, when selecting fabrics to upholster this quartet of shapely side chairs, the key was picking medium-scale prints with a central motif that could easily be centered on both a chair's back and seat. Reserve looser, more overall prints, such as the damask and paisley, for the shapelier frames. The boxier chairs got tighter, more geometric prints.

7

LESSON SEVEN
have fun with it

Pattern isn't just for window coverings, wall treatments, and upholstery. On the contrary, it can also be used to brighten plain white lampshades or add a dash of excitement to a simple chest of drawers. And why stop at one pattern? For added fun, you can mix patterns on the same object. The chest of drawers shown here owes its dynamic appearance to two botanical-print papers placed in an alternating fashion down its front.

no wallflowers
Red mats make the artwork take center stage.

a good fit
Tired of slouchy slipcovers? Look for designs with hook-and-loop tape (or add to your own cover) to hug curves and secure to the frame.

GETTING WARMER
test the waters with a few color changes

Ease into the idea of a color-infused home by making small changes that can be reversed after a few days if you're not thrilled. First, select a signature hue (we chose red), then follow our lead. Replace white lampshades with a more colorful design. Cover seating with neutral canvas slipcovers that have a contrasting welt, and toss bright pillows into the mix. Tweak artwork by adding colored mats. Finish by painting a part of the wall.

Start by selecting your accent color. Because the room is void of color, there's no way to go wrong. Simply select your favorite hue.

LIGHT IDEA
The white lampshades that came with our bottle-shape table lamps were too similar in color to the ceramic bases, so we reworked them, covering each with a jaunty red fabric. Wrapping the top and bottom opening of the shade with bright white seam binding tape (available at fabric stores) gives each a polished finish.

PILLOW TALK
Red pillows add a dash of excitement to the all-white sofa while calling attention to the cover's crisp red welting. And because pillows are readily available and easy to work with, don't be afraid to experiment. Bring home more than you think you'll need and try out several combinations before settling on a style.

PAINT POWER
Paint is one of the easiest ways to bring color into your home, but you don't have to cover every wall in intense color. Instead, highlight an architectural feature, such as the paneled insets here. If you find your walls lacking architectural detail, simulate the look: Mark off the design with painter's tape, then fill between the lines.

TESTING, TESTING
use these online sources to explore color schemes and options

① Color Visualizer
www.behr.com
Upload images of your rooms and test colors using Behr Paint's ColorSmart tool. You can choose a palette of colors yourself, or get color advice and options as you work with the tool.

② Color Matcher
www.benjaminmoore.com
Use your iPhone to match the color of any item with a paint color from Benjamin Moore with ben® Color Capture™, the iPhone color-matching app. Just snap a picture of any item, and ben finds the paint color.

③ Project Planner
www.dutchboy.com
Test a variety of paint combinations in sample rooms with Dutch Boy Paint's Color Simplicity Tool. Save the combinations you like best in a project folder.

be bold
Improve the atmosphere of an all-white room by painting the walls a hot hue.

JUST RIGHT
demonstrate your color courage

OK, you've lived with your small changes for a while and you really like the results. Now go all out. Paint every wall—or at least portions of them—a shade of your signature hue. Enhance your already dashing sofa and armchair by adding bold slipcovers on the seats. Finally, look to the floor. Replace the bland beige area rug with a patterned design that incorporates several shades of your primary color.

Solid planes of contrasting color make a room more dynamic. Incorporating patterns that play off your color theme enhances the effect.

EASY EXTRAS
Increase the color intensity by adding a few extra pillows to your seating. For maximum impact, you'll want to vary the shape, size, and color—perhaps even adding a pattern or additional accent color to the mix. As before, look for designs that incorporate the room's key colors, in this case beige and red.

COOLER COVER-UP
You've already given your white upholstery the slip, but why not increase the impact by dressing the seat cushions with covers made from a solid or patterned fabric? Simply select a color or design that coordinates with the rest of the room. Here, the striped fabric shown on the sofa inspired the orange on this armchair.

FUN UNDERFOOT
Still color-shy? Modular rugs, such as this one from InterfaceFlor that comes in 19½-inch squares you piece together, can be easily customized to fit your mood. Start with a basic beige design and add colored tiles as your confidence grows.

OPTIONS
see it differently

Do these ideas click for you but in a different hue? Not a problem—the color lessons here readily translate to any preferred color scheme.

brighten with blue?

opt for orange?

chapter
THREE

{ BEFORE & AFTER

case study

a girl can change her mind

Flexibility is key to Terri Klekner, who reimagines her California apartment once every few years by updating her old furniture and sprucing up with new paint.

THEN:
RED&
WHITE

NOW:
BLACK
&BEIGE

For Terri Klekner, sticking to one look for very long is, well, boring. But who has the budget for a total makeover every few years? Inside her San Diego apartment, Terri developed a strategy for flexibility early on. She first focused on investing in a few key, style-neutral pieces that would allow her to change the look of her place as her tastes evolved. Then, by combining a diverse mix of flea-market finds with classic furnishings and fabrics, she accumulated fill-in pieces she could parlay into an infinite number of looks.

Having redecorated her 1930s one-bedroom apartment twice before, Terri once again looked for change—this time trading out her red country French decor for something more streamlined and modern. "The old look was outdated, and I was getting tired of it," Terri says. She opted to create a "clean, simple style" that would help her small place look bigger. With just under 750 square feet of living space, Terri relied on her philosophy of choosing pieces she loves but limiting eclecticism. "Too many styles in an apartment looks like you have no plan. You should always have a plan," she says.

Her plan was to create a sleeker scheme with easy-to-alter pillows and bedding that would allow her to change the apartment's

1 RED, WHITE, AND TOILE
The shelving niche was formerly decked out in country French charm with warm floral prints and a cozy cottage side chair.

2 SWEET AS CAN BE
In the first look, the green painted cabinet anchored the hallway, supported by a sweet ensemble of roses, polka dots, and toile.

country french chic

table switcheroo:
Now used in the bedroom to store linens, the country pine trunk was originally a coffee table in the living room.

pillow power:
Before the serene redo, rich red toile coordinated with slipcovers and accent fabrics to create a country French motif.

sheer brilliance:
Tab-top curtains complemented the country look and balanced the bold-pattern accent pillows.

❝Comfort is really important to me; I'm constantly told how comfortable and inviting my home is.❞

— TERRI KLEKNER, homeowner

look seasonally and easily while leaving key furniture pieces in place. But doing away with the cozy country look didn't mean doing away with comfort. "Comfort is really important to me; I'm constantly told how comfortable and inviting my home is," Terri says. She maintained that coziness by keeping textiles, paint colors, and accessories simple but warm.

Knowing that she wanted to use some black furnishings this time around, Terri painted the walls a creamy color to help the dark pieces visually pop. "It's low in cost but big in change," she says of the paint. Terri then ripped up the gray wall-to-wall carpet to reveal well-preserved wood floors that add warmth to the small space. After a humorous (and rather disastrous) attempt at refinishing the floors herself, Terri hired a pro from a home improvement store to sand them. "What would have taken me a few weeks took him several hours and only cost $150," she says.

Next, Terri traded out the old tab-top sheers for streamlined draperies. She re-covered chairs in neutral fabrics. To stretch her budget, she shuffled the heavier, more rustic pieces of furniture into new roles. The most dramatic example is Terri's old coffee table (a country pine trunk), which she exchanged for a salvaged ottoman that she re-covered in leopard-print fabric. She also gave the cabinet, formerly painted with a green decorative finish, a facelift with a coat of glossy black paint.

By creating a neutral canvas on which updated furniture, classic fabrics, and sophisticated accessories can shine, Terri has given her cozy one-bedroom a new lease on life.

1 SMALL CHANGE, BIG IMPACT Sculptural accents such as shells, glassware, and a large wooden "T" bring a sophisticated new look to the shelving niche.

2 A BREATH OF FRESH AIR Cool colors and clean-lined pieces, led by the newly painted black cabinet, give the hallway a tailored, more modern look.

sophisticated details

upscale table:
For dual function in a small space, Terri reupholstered a salvaged ottoman that now doubles as a chic and spacious coffee table.

fresh pillows:
By keeping her sofa but switching to soft accent pillows, Terri was able to create a more sophisticated look.

serene curtains:
Using the existing rod, Terri updated the old country tab-top curtains to a more streamlined ring-and-clip style.

> "Too many styles in an apartment looks like you have no plan. You should always have a plan."
> — TERRI KLEKNER

GET THE FEEL OF IT
changing looks with a few details

Pattern and texture were vital to both apartment makeovers. In her previous country French decor, Terri chose wicker accents and bold patterned fabrics such as toile to set a color-cozy mood. With her new, more modern sensibility, she opted for streamlined finishes and smooth, supple fabrics, including more solids, for a tailored look.

1 GOURMET DELIGHT
Bright red jars and accessories matched the red toile accents throughout Terri's apartment.

2 BRIGHT WORK ZONE
Terri's work space was previously decorated with warm wooden details, including a collage frame, tabletop, and brown corkboard.

3 COZY NEST
Terri's old bedroom had a bolder palette with rich crimson walls and red toile accents on her chair, headboard, pillows, and comforter.

4 DRAPED EFFECT
To match the eclectic, found-object look of country French, Terri opted for a basic wooden shelf draped with fabric to store clothing and laundry.

① KITCHEN COLLAGE
Metal utility shelves are stocked with woven baskets to reduce visual clutter and hide linens and other kitchen accessories.

② CORNER OFFICE
A black-and-white photograph of Paris was the inspiration for Terri's work space, now decorated with more modern accessories.

③ ROOM WITH A VIEW
Terri's bedroom is now a calming cream color with white linens that create a fresh look.

④ OPEN-AND-SHUT CASE
Instead of wicker baskets and toile storage boxes, Terri's clothing is now stored in a classic armoire stained a rich walnut color that will surely make the next transition.

CLEAN & SIMPLE COLOR
from cozy country to classic modern

Part of what drives Terri's new decor is its precise color scheme. Soft taupe, white, metallics, and dramatic black set a subtle palette and signal the style shift from the busy red, brown, and white that filled the space before. The best part about Terri's new look? Flexibility. It goes beautifully with everything she already had.

*Paneled walls: a little drywall'll do ya!

*Windows too small for the fab view. Replace with French doors.

from shack to chic

Since the 1950s, this tiny Florida home has given young families a start. In making it their own, the Ross family updated it for the next generation.

Generations of visitors to central Florida's Lake Butler aren't fools. One look at the clear blue water and white-sand beach, and they start planning a way to extend their stay. In the 1960s, Jim Ross's parents were no different. They spent many weekends on the shore at a small, unassuming fishing camp.

Over time, they built a full-time home nearby. Jim grew up on the lake, and he couldn't imagine staking his own claim anywhere else. Fortunately, his parents still owned the fishing camp. "This was the place where people lived while they built their better home down the road," Jim says of the humble two-bedroom cottage.

An architectural designer, Jim had the ideas, muscle, and skill to update the house, which he acquired from his parents. He devoted evenings and weekends to hammering, salvaging, and scrapping until the house resembled his vision: a whimsical waterfront home with a casual attitude.

Retaining the home's original footprint, Jim added an airy upper level with a master suite and porch that capture the view. Downstairs, he freshened the existing room arrangement with new flooring and wall treatments and large windows.

But Jim admits that decorating didn't really start until he met his wife, Jennifer, a few years ago. They shopped for furniture together, cultivating a Caribbean-plantation scheme, and she suggested the earthy paint hues that capitalize on the sunshine and shift in color as the day wears on.

Right now, however, the Rosses have their hands full. Daughter Delanie was born just a week after these photos were taken, and, for the first time since Jim bought the house, the projects have ceased. Jim and Jennifer feel the house has finally reached its potential: It still has the lake-house charm that lured Jim's parents, and now, fully updated, it will shelter this young family through the start of their lives together.

before

after

GETTING INTO CHARACTER
The original house, *far left*, lacked character and color. Jim and Jennifer Ross, *above*, changed all that by remodeling the house, *left*, in the bright hues and fanciful details of Victorian houses in the Florida Keys, as well as the open-air porches and tin roofs of older central Florida cottages.

GOOD WILL

WREN
FLORIDA CITRUS FRUITS
R.D. KEENE, INC.
WINTER GARDEN, FLA.

FLORIDA CITRUS FRUITS
ILDEE BRAND

fun, fast, fabulous

juicy fruit
Jim Ross's family business is oranges. He turned an old citrus crate into a table and framed vintage crate labels as easy wall art.

pillow bright
A dark leather sofa is durable, but the hue can get heavy. Pump it up with bright, low-cost pillows from a decor store.

save face
Recall the Before view on page 80? The Ross's covered old paneling with a thin brick veneer and grout. Voilà! Aging with grace.

GOOD HOME   Dennis Wedlick

ROSS GROVES

MAKE-DO OR REDO?

1 TILE AISLE
Custom tile costs a boatload. The make-do? Jim bought two colors of ceramic floor tile in bulk from a home center, then laid his own checkerboard floor. He and Jennifer made the fish backsplash from broken tiles.

2 RACK 'EM UP
Blank walls can mean untapped space. The redo? Jim cut in niches for extra storage, such as the wine bottle holder he created by stacking clay drainage tile tubes unearthed from the back yard.

3 ISLAND IDEAL
The Rosses' kitchen is too small for even a small island. The make-do? A petite wooden wine cart that serves as shelving, towel bar, and extra counter space.

before

before

WELCOME TO THE FUTURE
The pine-paneled cabinets and ancient appliances, *far left*, made the kitchen the top candidate for an upgrade. The long living room/dinette/kitchen was dark—and the fireplace, *left*, anything but a focal point. Rather than rip it out, Jim cleaned the stone and added a new white mantel. Light paint hues and tile brightened the mood.

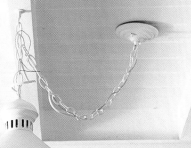

BRUSH UP
The Rosses found pineapple-motif dining chairs that fit the tropical vibe, but the off-white finish didn't match their table. The fix? They painted the table base to match. White-painted ceiling beams reflect sunlight through the room.

Rafters and upper-level
windows dressed with
plantation shutters give
the bath architectural
character.

SUITE SMART

1 HIDE & SEEK
Shutters hide the TV and DVD player. Jim faced the fireplace in leftover tile from the kitchen floor— lots less expensive than marble.

2 CEILING SMART
Rope lights hidden in the molding cast soft illumination from an elaborate ceiling in the master bedroom. "I tend to focus attention on the ceiling in a bedroom, where you actually pay attention to it," Jim says.

3 POINT OF VIEW
A spacious porch with terrific views of Lake Butler awaits just through the French doors in the master bedroom. Fish brackets on the porch post are a reminder of the home's original use.

4 VANITY'S SAKE
At a home center, Jim found vanities that look like old dressers for a more furnished look.

SHOP SMART

FRUGAL FOR THE FUTURE
saving in order to splurge (wisely)

Jim introduced Jennifer to the warehouses, closeout sales, and home centers that he stalks for bargains. "I just don't like to pay retail if I don't have to," he says. That frugality afforded them master-suite upgrades—replacing carpet with wood floors and installing a steam shower and claw-foot bathtub—that are sure to pay off in resale value.

Bland walls, a bitsy kitchen, and quirky crannies—the joys of apartment living! But this plucky Maryland renter found bright, inexpensive, low-commitment ways to style her space.

make it
your own

the building

* Ugh! White walls! Juicy orange paint will liven these up.

* Two not-quite-matching bookcases will flank this odd bump-out nicely.

* This bookcase is not built-in—it's the land-lord's. Out it goes.

* A pair of thin sisal rugs will soften these hardwood floors.

RENTAL RESCUE
Temporary digs can serve
up just as much style as a
home you own. Just use
smart tactics that deliver a
lot of punch for your penny.
A sunny hue replaces rental
white on these walls, and
artwork—at every turn
here—only requires a bit of
spackle and touch-up paint
when you leave.

Real-Life Living Room

Neutral Zone
A classic white-denim sofa is a decorating chameleon: It can slip seamlessly into any decor, no matter the style, with perfect grace.

To the Letter
Among renter Kara Norman's favorite items to collect are old sign letters. She hangs them on walls or displays them as freestanding sculpture.

No More Blinds
White metal blinds are a dreaded apartment staple. This matchstick window shade is a richly textured upgrade at the right retail price.

Check It Out
Kara found the curtain fabric marked down at a discount fabric store. "It was a bargain and happened to go with everything," she says.

Aah, the double-edged sword of renting an apartment. On the one hand, you're not responsible for replacing leaky pipes or shelling out property taxes. But on the other, you're at the mercy of your landlord's taste in decorating. Or are you?

One creative gal, Kara Norman, persuaded her landlord to let her fix up her one-bedroom apartment in Frederick, Maryland (about 50 miles outside Washington, D.C.). Kara's ingenuity, thrift, and eye for arranging are inspirational to any renter or homeowner whose place could use a perk-up.

Take the living room. White walls and poor sunlight gave way to summery orange paint. Two sisal rugs soften the hardwood floors and define areas for the neutral-color furnishings. A pair of armchairs (antique store finds from San Antonio) is dressed in the original muslin, which is meant to be covered with fabric of the owner's choice. "But I like the muslin just fine," Kara says. She added rope trim to make the chairs look more finished and to hide the staples in the fabric. A white-denim sofa with classic lines and an upholstered footrest/coffee table offer plenty of casual seating.

"I change my mind a lot, so having neutral furnishings just makes sense so that everything else can change around them," she says.

ORANGE TANGO
For the north-facing living room, *left*, Kara Norman chose orange sherbet-color paint because she "wanted something warm and colorful to make up for the fact that it doesn't get great sun."

HER DOMAIN
Kara, *above right*, smiles from her second-floor apartment window.

MASTER OF ARTS
This bookcase, *right*, stashes Kara's books and serves as a display ledge for art.

TRADING SPACES
An auction find, this black sideboard, *far right*, has been versatile. "I have had it in every room of my house except the kitchen and bathroom," Kara says.

before

EATING IN
The tiny kitchen, *above left*, includes a pair of armchairs, a half-round table, and an old chalkboard as art. Kara splurged on the chairs, which are wider than most kitchen chairs. "You want to be comfortable sitting everywhere, in every room," she says.

SPACE ECONOMICS
The kitchen is highly efficient: A basket, *left*, corrals canisters, and a fabric screen hides the radiator.

PAINT POWER
With permission, Kara refreshed the kitchen cabinets, *right*, with white and gray paint. "I painted the lower cabinets slightly darker so the range sticks out less," she says. New hardware helped, too. "I'm forever changing knobs on stuff," Kara says.

The tiny kitchen, however, presented a monster-size challenge. "There's all of three feet of counter space," Kara says, plus a radiator, a harvest-gold range, and countertops that had seen better days. Concealing these flaws required a fabric screen (for the radiator), two shades of paint (for the cabinets), and a butcher-block cutting board (for the countertop).

In her bedroom, Kara kept the white space from fading into blandness by introducing texture and doses of black for drama. A $5 tag-sale chair is a homey accent, and a slim-line bamboo table fits snugly next to the bed.

Her place's cozy size put Kara's design prowess to the test with great results. "I think a lot of people these days are looking for bigger houses, but not me," she says. "There is a size that's too small, certainly, but I can keep this place clean, I know where everything is, and I don't make as many stupid buying decisions because not everything will fit! I'm much happier in a smaller place."

Clever Kitchen

Use Every Inch
A hook below the sink holds a dish towel. In this crowded kitchen, every sliver of space counts. "You've gotta pack it in," Kara says.

A Place for All
Woven-grass totes are stylish storage bins. "There was height above the cabinets I wanted to utilize, but I wanted it to look nice," Kara says.

Home Plate
A large white platter slides over to disguise the outlet behind the faucet. Kara added a vintage sconce to shed some light on the countertop.

Savvy Concealer
Kara covered the worn countertop with a lip-front cutting board. "You wouldn't even know that the countertop is disgusting," she says.

Budget-Wise Bedroom

Smart Substitute
An old picture frame, which Kara picked up at an antiques shop, fills in as a headboard and adds color to the bedroom's white scheme.

On the Cheap
The big toile pillow cost next to nothing: Both sides are discontinued fabric samples Kara sewed together and stuffed with polyfill.

Calming Curtain
Airy drifts of white linen—bought for only $3 per yard—hang from ring clips on a curtain rod to create a dreamy backdrop for the bed.

Two-Sided Throw
Crafted of leopard-print fleece on one side and black-and-white toile on the other, this reversible throw can make the room sassy or classy.

before

before

*RENT CONTROL
tricks for apartment dwellers

PAINT After receiving permission from your landlord, use paint as a quick cosmetic cure-all for walls, cabinets, and built-ins.

WINDOW TREATMENTS Removing the standard metal blinds and putting up store-bought or hand-sewn curtains is a huge step toward a friendly, personalized space.

NEUTRAL FURNITURE Invest in pieces that suit a variety of color schemes and transcend trends so you're free to experiment often.

SMALL RUGS A few sisal rugs in smaller (4 × 6- and 5 × 8-foot) sizes can be configured to fit almost any room—and they're portable.

WHITE WONDER
The white scheme in Kara's bedroom, *left*, is far from bland or boring. She included black accents, such as the checked bed skirt and toile pillow, and items with interesting texture, such as the bamboo end table and sisal rug.

A SMALL FORTUNE
Window shutters give the bathroom, *above*, privacy. The sink cabinet is hidden under toile fabric that was a price splurge. ("Go for the gusto if it's something puny!" Kara says of its price.)

HALL OF FAME
Bold letters are graphic statements for awkwardly sized walls in the hallway, *right*. Soft pink paint warms the space without overwhelming it, while a chandelier on a dimmer switch "gives it a little sparkle," Kara says.

new look, same stuff

Yes, old furniture can learn new tricks. See how fabric and paint reinvent furnishings so they roll with changes in personal style—and homes—over time.

the exterior of
the house today

the ottoman
in 1990s floral

WHY BUY NEW WHEN OLD WILL DO?
The Livseys' house in Fort Leavenworth,
Kansas, *inset top*, has been home to many
famous generals in its 164-year history—
among them George Custer and Colin Powell.
All interiors on post are painted white, so
Keri Livsey co-opted the clean look for herself,
adding color through accent pieces. In the
piano room, *this photo*, as in the rest of the
house, she swears by white cotton slipcovers
to unite and update old pieces, including a
formerly floral ottoman, *inset above*.

the chairs in
1990s stripe

the Livseys on
their porch

IN EVERY HOUSE: A NEW CHALLENGE
A pair of armchairs purchased in 1993 for
$12 and $15, *top*, received a style update
with fresh tan fleur-de-lis upholstery,
opposite, to fit the airy yet classic look of
the Livseys' latest home on post. Keri and
her family—husband Tim and children
Sam and Hannah, *inset above*—are
experienced movers, thanks to Tim's
Army career.

A master at reimagining her look to
suit each new house, Keri Livsey has
discovered that the key to making old
furniture look new is a coat of paint
and some fabric. If you doubt Keri's
mastery of the science of repurposing, check her credentials: six moves in
10 years to locations stateside and abroad, thanks to the Army career of her
husband, Brig. Gen. (Ret.) Tim Livsey. Keri's abilities were put to the test in
this home in Fort Leavenworth, Kansas. "My look is my look," she says. "I'd
never buy a whole suite of matching furniture. I want to make it mine."

The nomadic nature of Army life suits Keri just fine. "I love that
challenge of figuring out where to put things in each house, the puzzle,"
she says. "I'm constantly editing and filtering pieces through. I don't
reinvent every time." If she's missing key elements, she shops local garage
sales, antiques malls, and flea markets for pieces to complete the decor.
House sizes vary from post to post, so an old find that won't fit in the new
house is simply sold at the next garage sale. How many pieces has she
recycled this way? "Lord only knows!" Keri says. "The good thing is that
almost every post has a spring and fall postwide garage sale, and the entire
community comes out for it."

Keri sees other benefits in moving so frequently: One is the
transformation of her personal style. "My houses have constantly evolved,"
she says. "I've grown a lot. Like everyone, you start with a smaller budget . . .
and grow from there." The second benefit is that because the military
will pay to move only a certain weightload of belongings, Keri is forced to
choose only multipurpose, budget-friendly furnishings. "For big pieces, I
never pay over $100," she says. "You wouldn't believe how many dressers
and beds I have bought for $5, $10, or $15 tops."

Raised in Oskaloosa, Iowa, in a family of teachers and creative types, Keri
was deeply influenced by her mother's ability to create "something from
nothing," as Keri says, by taking auction finds and rehabbing them into
beautiful decorative elements. Keri tried the teaching field but decided it
wasn't for her, choosing instead to tap her innate decorative sensibilities to
help other military wives create stylish homes using stuff they already own.

Always ready for the next adventure (and the next opportunity to
repurpose stuff), Keri is already planning for her next move—off post this
time, because Tim is retiring. "I'm going to make my next house more
sophisticated," she says. "I got this awesome black tufted leather ottoman
off the Internet for a great price. I'm going to base my whole look on it."
And the Livsey kids, 9-year-old twins Hannah and Sam, want their say as
well: "They've already asked if they can decorate their own rooms in the
next house. They're getting old enough to do it now. I've created a couple
of little monsters, I think!" Keri says with a laugh.

MOVES

1 NEUTRALIZE KEY PIECES
"You can always change pillows and accessories to add color," Keri Livsey says. She prefers white slipcovered furniture because a dash of bleach easily takes care of stains.

2 KEEP THINGS ORGANIZED
"Keep nothing that you really don't need or use," she says. "Have a place for everything and keep it there."

3 STARTING OVER IS OVERRATED
"My furniture ends up in different rooms from house to house," she says. "It could be a buffet in one house, a dresser in another." Keri looks for furnishings that are flexible enough to transition.

ADDING CASUAL STYLE TO A FORMAL SPACE
In the dining room, *this photo*, Keri added
springtime touches of green and lavender. In fall,
she swaps them out for richer accents. *Top row,
from left:* Embroidered napkins embellish the
backs of the chairs. Keri uses her grandmother's
shell collection to anchor a vase of hydrangeas. A
whimsical place setting lends a casual look to the
formal table that came with the house.

the buffet
before paint,
early 1990s

the chairs sans
slipcovers, 2001

JUST A LITTLE PAINT AND FABRIC
The buffet, *top*, purchased at an auction
for $10 and then cleaned up, was a
wedding gift to Tim and Keri from her
parents. Keri eventually gave the stained
buffet a whitewash, *left*, to suit her
casual country look. A lattice leaned
against the top provides an interesting
spot to hang a picture. The dining chairs,
above, came from a garage sale for $60
(which also included a table, not shown)
and were painted to mask the low-
quality wood. Keri slipcovered them,
left, for protection from sticky hands
(and a new look).

"My look is my look. I'd never buy a whole suite of matching furniture. I want to make it mine."

—KERI LIVSEY, homeowner

EVERYTHING IS ALL-WHITE
Keri pulled the home's all-white color scheme into the guest room, *opposite*, adding touches of soft pastel colors in small accessories. The iron bed was passed down from Keri's mom. It's been spray-painted green, black, chrome, and white in its past.

Make It Your Own

Get Creative
Look for new ways to use old things. Keri Livsey hangs fabric and ribbons on curtain rods over a window in her laundry room, *opposite*.

Reinterpret
Don't be afraid to change a piece. Keri has painted her dining table three times to keep up with her house and style.

Go for more
Multipurpose. Keri found two metal planters—one holds plants, the other is used as a large ice chest for entertaining.

Embrace change
Your tastes may change, and that's OK. Over the years, Keri has updated some sentimental pieces and thrown away fad items.

Embellish
Keri adds her own decorative touches to plain white napkins with embroidery and to picture frames with white or colored paint.

the goods

furniture
FIRST+AID

Yes, these thrift shop pieces are in critical condition, but a few days in intensive care will revive their style and dramatically increase their life expectancy.

FINE DINING
fresh white paint reveals chic casual style

High style often lurks just beneath the surface of outdated furniture. The fretwork of these dining chairs offered modern appeal that was spoiled by its muddy fruitwood finish. All this dining set needed to shine was a light sanding, a coat of good primer, and a couple of coats of white semigloss paint. Before painting, we removed the dated decorative medallions from the table legs and filled the holes with wood filler. The upholstery—in a pattern that mirrors the fretwork—was an inexpensive fabric store find. Dining chair seats typically detach with a few twists of a screwdriver, and reupholstery is simple to tackle with a bit of fresh foam and a heavy-duty staple gun.

the before

+

paint

the solution

=

the after

SAVE A SEAT
fresh white paint reveals chic casual style

These terrific little chairs had everything going for them—well, almost everything. Their lines were elegant, they were as sturdy as the day they were made, and they were diminutive enough to nestle perfectly into corners. Unfortunately, the avocado and gold upholstery was a throwback to 1968, and the legs were painted green to match. We stripped, sanded, and wiped the legs with a nearly opaque stain because the wood grain wasn't worth highlighting. Two coats of polyurethane sealed the legs, and the chairs were ready for the upholsterer. We chose solid velvet for the shells and striped velvet on the inside backs to call attention to the chairs' alluring lines.

the before

+

the solution

=

the after

the before

+

the solution

=

the after

NEW MEDIA
recycling extends beyond papers and cans

The most exciting furniture makeovers create innovative new functions for tired old pieces. This vaguely Scandinavian-style dresser had great lines and dramatic wood veneer, but the beauty had been battered out of it. Fortunately, the flat drawers were a snap to strip with a rotary sander. With a little wood conditioner, some teak stain, and a couple of coats of polyurethane, the drawers were finished in just a few hours. The dresser's chipped and stained shell presented a bigger challenge. Sturdy vinyl wallcovering proved to be the perfect cover-up, and it mimicked the look of expensive linen-covered furniture. The horizontal supports between drawers were painted to match. Creating a niche for a DVD player was as simple as removing a drawer, popping off the drawer rail, and cutting a small hole in the back for cords. New legs, found online, lower the height and update the look.

chapter
FOUR

BUYMANSHIP

- **CASE STUDY:**
  I Only Buy if It's on Sale

- **How to Buy Sofas**

- **How to Buy Tables**

- **How to Buy Rugs**

I only buy if it's on sale

Ever fallen in love with a piece in a decorating magazine only to be crushed moments later by a phrase like "custom-designed," "to-the-trade-only," or "18th-century antique"? It's a total bummer, we know. But this is *not* one of those stories. This is a story about a stay-at-home mom named Maggie Jensen who shops like the rest of us—one sale at a time, every season of the year. Maggie makes retail look remarkable, and she'll show you how.

$50
linen drapery panels
Discovered at the Restoration Hardware outlet store.

$400
pine dining set
Snatched it up online so fast . . . source forgotten!

$600
pine armoire
Carted it home from Costco.

quick change

Make your room look its seasonal best.

FALL

WINTER

The secrets to seasonal decor
how to make a neutral scheme sing in all seasons (for just cents)

Maggie Jensen advocates simplicity, but not when it comes to decorating for the holidays. "I love Easter, Halloween, and Christmas," she says. Because her rooms are clean and neutral, it's easy to integrate special-occasion details, no matter the season.

HER BUDGET-SAVVY SECRETS
Buy seasonal decor, ribbons, dinnerware, and embellishments at deep after-season discounts and scour sale racks year-round for items in your holiday colors. For example, black-and-white gingham ribbon looks bewitching; red glassware rings Christmas.

GETTING THE HARVEST LOOK
For a fun harvest look that works for both Halloween and Thanksgiving, this hot-glue mama used silk harvest leaves, papier-mâché mini pumpkins and gourds, and jaunty black-and-white-checked ribbon to adorn her Home Depot chandelier in the eating area of the kitchen, *opposite*. She also made easy ribbon, pinecone, and leaf dangles for chair backs, and used pumpkins and squash as bright seasonal color for the table here and in the dining room. Leafy branch clippings fill a vase on the family room console.

GETTING THE CHRISTMAS LOOK
At Christmastime, Maggie makes a quick change to red and chartreuse, *above*. Pearly glass balls threaded onto bright green ribbon ties dangle from the chandelier, bedecked with fragrant fresh greens. A simple evergreen wreath hangs on the door with a fanciful chartreuse bow; and a pair of stacked glass cake plates dressed with evergreens, glass balls, pinecones, and red berries makes a sophisticated, no-fuss centerpiece. Red-velvet slipcovers and red stemware create added beauty and richness.

$150
wall mirror
Eyed this sparkling
beauty at
Z Gallerie.

$700
leather club
chair pair
Snapped them up
at Costco.

$100
sea-grass
cube ottoman
Clicked this online
find into the cart.

RETAIL-O-RAMA
A World Market table, Z Gallerie mirror,
candlesticks from Ross, striped vases from
the former Marshall Field's online, and a
wood vase from a Salvation Army thrift
store lend sophistication to the family
room. Pottery Barn pillows on chairs from
Costco provide a hint of pattern atop a
rug from The Home Depot.

Where the boys are
a room that grows with the kids and doesn't cost much

How does a bargain-hound mom make a cool boys' room, *below*, without cracking the piggy bank?

1. KEEP COLORS KID-CHIC Navy, white, and red are kid-friendly and easy to coordinate from wall to bed to accessories to floor. And they're so ageless, they won't go out of favor anytime soon.

2. PINE AWAY Hey, pine is a great-looking wood for way less. These IKEA pine beds? $80 each.

3. SAVE TO SPLURGE With savings on beds,

Maggie bought Tommy Hilfiger tropical comforters at Macy's (yep, she went during a sale) for pattern.

4. USE YOUR OWN GEAR Scott Jensen's college-era surfboards are now a part of the boys' decor. He and Jake grab 'em for father-son surfing lessons.

5. PICK A COLOR POP Maggie chose red as the accent color to carry the eye around the room. She got bright red blankets, lampshades, a trophy shelf, and each of the boys' initials.

KID CLEVER.
The boys' red, white, and blue scheme is yet another chameleon against which lots of accents will look great as the boys grow.

KID SMART

> "When you keep things neutral, you can get a great basic look that dresses up nicely with accessories."
>
> —MAGGIE JENSEN

SOFA STYLES

1 **SOFT AND COZY**
Kick back and relax on a Lawson, which has straight arms that are lower than the back (perfect for napping). Loose cushions are comfy; firm cushions are ideal for conversation.

2 **SLEEK SOPHISTICATE**
Clean lines make the tuxedo modern, which has flat arms the same height as the back. Without back pillows, the sofa is a regal entertaining spot; with them, it's a casual reading nook.

3 **CLASSIC COMFORT**
A mainstay in sofa design is the rolled arm, the perfect place to lay your head or a spot to sit during a party. Use care when measuring—the arms add extra inches to the sofa's length.

After several years of living with hand-me-down and "make-do" furniture, you're ready to take the plunge and buy a grown-up sofa for your grown-up home. But purchasing such a big-ticket item has your stomach in knots. Where do you start?

How do you distinguish quality from junk? What's a fair price? Which upholstery fabric will stand the test of time (and your children and pets)? How do you find something attractive without falling for a passing trend?

Before shelling out hundreds or even thousands on a "real" sofa, follow these tips for getting a quality piece at a good price that will last for many years.

● ASK YOURSELF how you will use your sofa. Knowing whether you want to get lost in the sofa's cushions, sit upright to entertain, or fall somewhere in between will help you whittle the many style options down to just a few. Your lifestyle will also narrow down fabric choices (slick silk isn't smart for the kids-and-pets set, for example).

● MEASURE YOUR SPACE and lay down newspapers to get a better view of how much sofa your room can handle. Settle on a realistic budget. These factors will reduce the temptation to fall in love with a too-large or too-expensive beauty.

● STUDY UP ON SOFA CONSTRUCTION and upholstery, then ask your salesperson lots of questions. Be sure to inquire about available warranties and stain treatments. He or she will take you more seriously, and you won't have buyer's remorse later. Also ask how long the floor model has been on display; even the firmest sofa will get squishy after hundreds of customers have tested it out.

● HAVE FUN! With a friend in tow, hit the furniture stores. Take your favorite sofas for a test drive—climb aboard and get comfy. Grab the arms and back, which shouldn't wiggle, and pick up one end to be certain the sofa is sturdy and doesn't sag.

● IF YOUR DREAM SOFA is available only through an out-of-town retailer, you can purchase online. But it's wise to take a trip to the retailer to try it before committing.

● FINALLY, HOLD YOUR HORSES. If you're lucky and find an in-stock sofa you love, you may be able to take it home that day. Most orders, particularly a specific upholstery request, can take several weeks or even months for delivery.

high-low

Make the most of your investment by purchasing the best-quality sofa you can afford. High-quality sofas are made of kiln-dried hardwood, hardwood plywood, or steel. They have eight-way, hand-tied coils or steel-spring construction, are screwed and glued at all joints, and have wrapped-foam cushions with at least 1.8 density. Lower-quality sofas are made of wood-and-plastic composites or conventional plywood, have fewer springs that are not reinforced, use staples to hold support blocks or have no blocks at all, and have low-density unwrapped foam cushions. Ask your salesperson about the sofa's construction and then take it for a spin (sit on it, lie down in a variety of positions, and bounce a bit to check the suspension). And don't skimp on cushion quality—it is one of the greatest measures of overall sofa comfort and quality. Down and feather cushions are considered supreme for their quality and longevity, but they add considerable cost.

4 **SHAPELY BEAUTY**
Although it is not known for its comfort, the camelback (aka Chippendale) is certainly the most graceful. It has an arced back, curved arms, and a tight back (no pillows).

5 **BITS AND PIECES**
For ultimate flexibility and versatility, choose a sectional sofa. The modular system offers myriad configurations, from a simple chair to a large sleeper sofa coupled with a recliner.

6 **MODERN APPEAL**
The minimalist armless sofa is an entertainer's dream. Given its super slim profile, it seats a surprisingly large number of people comfortably in its minimal space.

When choosing a sofa, let function dictate form. If entertaining is your thing, choose a sofa that encourages conversation. Pick a narrow sofa with an upright back, firm seat, and few or no pillows. If you look forward each day to plopping down on the sofa to relax, look for one that feels more like a bed. Find a deeper sofa with plenty of cushy pillows (down-stuffed cushions are particularly cozy).

SOLUTION SOFAS

Corner unit A small or unusually shaped room requires clever space planning. Make use of square footage by choosing a sectional sofa that includes a corner piece (often with underseat storage). This smart option captures an underutilized area without intruding into the room.

Sleeper Even if you don't have a dedicated guest room, you don't need to turn away overnight visitors. Invest in a sofa with a pullout bed to maximize space. A quality sleeper sofa has the look and feel of a traditional sofa, but concealed within its framework is a full- or queen-size bed.

Slipcovered Children and pets can wreak havoc on a sofa, but never fear—slipcovers are here. Just remove the cover and throw it in the wash. They're also a great way to seasonally change your decor or to keep up with color trends. Slipcover styles range from overstuffed to unfussy.

Chaise longue A chaise looks like a backless sofa with one arm. The elegant design is perfect for an open floor plan, where a full-size, tall-back sofa would obstruct views. Another benefit is that a chaise weighs less than a sofa, making it portable for use in multiple spaces.

Futon While a futon may not have the classic structure of a sleeper sofa, its hidden bed is typically more comfortable. A futon's construction and thicker mattress reduce bar-in-the-back syndrome. As a bonus, futon covers are easy to remove and clean or replace.

Settee A small room can be completely consumed by even an average-size sofa, which is typically at least 6 feet long. A space-saving alternative is a compact settee, which provides comfortable seating for two or three.

pros and cons of 5 popular upholstery fabrics

Leather
The most durable upholstery option, good-quality leather can last 15 years—twice as long as cloth. It is easy to clean with a vacuum or a damp cloth. Pet owners beware: Without proper treatment, leather is susceptible to scratches and discoloration.

Silk
Although its elegance and beauty make it a tempting choice, parents and pet owners should steer clear of delicate silk. The luxurious fabric is best suited for a showpiece sofa in a low-traffic area. Silk should always be lined and must be professionally cleaned.

Cotton
The old standby for soft and comfortable sofas is cotton upholstery. The natural fiber is strong and durable, especially when treated with a stain guard. Cotton comes in a variety of forms, including twill and denim; choose a textured fabric in a darker color to camouflage wear and stains.

Microsuede
The hottest trend in upholstery is microsuede, a synthetic fiber that mimics suede. This soft yet tough fabric is extremely durable, practically stain-resistant, easy to clean, and quite affordable. Plus, it is now available in a variety of textures and patterns.

Indoor-outdoor
Whether your sofa is on an all-season porch or sits by a window, cover it with indoor-outdoor fabric for durability. The fade- and stain-resistant fabric is a smart choice for children and pets. It comes in a variety of styles, including this soft yet strong chenille.

HOW TO BUY
tables

* The dining table is the hub of a home's activity, where a family eats, plays games, pays bills, and does homework. Choosing a table that handles what your life dishes out is simply a matter of taste and space.

SHAPE UP
Sure, a dining table is all about function, but don't dismiss its form. Choose a table with an interesting shape such as a pedestal style, *this photo*, a trestle style, *opposite bottom*, or one with turned legs, *opposite top*.

SUIT YOUR STYLE
From modern to country, there is a table to suit your design style. This sleek and modern table is fashioned from solid walnut and expands to seat 10. For cottage charm, opt for sturdy rattan painted an antique white hue, *opposite*.

TABLE TIPS

1 SHAPE
Rectangular and round tables are time-honored choices that fit most spaces. For a modern look, choose a square table. To add dimension in a boxy room, pick an oval or octagonal table.

2 STYLE
Rich wood finishes are classic, painted tables appear casual, and stainless steel looks modern. Carved legs are traditional, pedestals can be cottagey, and trestles are a farmhouse favorite.

3 SIZE
The ideal dining table hosts guests but doesn't overstuff the room. A big room? Get a large table that won't float in the space. Tiny room? Find a small table with leaves that double its capacity.

Expected to be a versatile workhorse, the dining table hosts dinner parties or poker games and acts as a makeshift office—or an art studio for your kids. It serves as the centerpiece of the dining room and needs to look stylish, too. Buying a dining table is a true test of form versus function. To get a piece that will look great and withstand the test of time, follow these tips.

- CONSIDER HOW YOU WILL USE THE TABLE. For example, if you host the entire family for Thanksgiving, you'll want a table that is expandable with leaves. If you are more interested in quiet conversation, choose a round table that allows everyone to see each other and converse easily. Square or round tables offer ultimate flexibility— intimate when closed yet expandable into a rectangle or oval for larger entertaining.
- MEASURE YOUR DINING ROOM. For maximum chair maneuvering and people passage, leave about 3 feet between the table and the walls. Allow for this space when determining how much table your room can handle.
- TAKE A SEAT AT EVERY TABLE. Test for comfort and stability. Be sure the table has enough elbow room (ideally allow about 30 inches between chair centers for each guest and across the table) but isn't so unwieldy that passing dishes is impossible. Lean on the table from all angles to check for wobbling.
- TEST THE TABLE WITH THE CHAIRS. If found separately, make sure the chairs, including arms, fit under the table. The arms shouldn't bump the table. Sit down and cross your legs—there should be space between the apron and your thighs. Also, check under the table to be sure the legs don't interfere with the chairs.
- PLACE YOUR ORDER—AND WAIT. If you buy an as-is or in-stock table from a local retailer, you may be able to take it home that day. Special orders for pieces with custom details or finishes and online purchases can take two weeks to two months.
- ASK ABOUT DELIVERY OPTIONS. Unless you buy a small, assemble-it-yourself table, it may be worth a small fee to have a pro haul and set up your purchase.

spacesavers

A hulking table can swallow a space, especially in a home without a dedicated dining room. Conquer small quarters with smart design:

PEEKABOO For all the benefits of an expandable table without the hassle of clunky leaves, invest in a table with self-storing leaves, *top*. This table reveals pop-up leaves that lock into place when needed.

DOUBLE DUTY In a combined living-dining room, opt for dual purpose with a cocktail table that rises to dining table height. Or pick a drop-leaf console table, *above*.

4 FUNCTION
Choose a table according to your life. Have children? Skip glass tops in favor of a pine piece that hides scratches. Live in a small loft? Buy a convertible coffee table that rises to dining height.

5 FINISH
Know your tolerance for wear. Glossy sheens and dark stains or paints show nicks faster; light woods and distressed finishes disguise it. Ask about watertight coatings to avoid water rings.

RUG RULES

1 Use a rug you love to inspire the whole look and color scheme of a room.

2 Be brave: Pick a rug with personality, and let it be artwork on the floor.

3 Size is important, so measure your space before making your final rug choice.

4 Exposing too much floor around the rug's edge can seem to shrink a room.

If you feel that a rug would limit your creativity, check into modular carpet tiles. The pre-cut squares often mix and match and are repositionable and replaceable as needed.

go **mod**ular

The first step in buying a new rug is to decide what type of fiber will best suit your needs. For example, is the new rug going under a dining table? Then you'll want one that is easy to clean.

Follow our handy guide below to pick the right rug fiber for your home.

• COTTON: Relatively inexpensive, cotton rugs are easy to clean, easy to dye, and extremely soft. Because the fibers are softer and more scuffable, they are best suited for scatter rugs or low-traffic areas like bedrooms.

• WOOL: More expensive than cotton, wool rugs are very durable, with little tendency to crush. They resist soil, but stains require professional cleaning, so they're best for low- to medium-traffic areas like bedrooms and living rooms.

• ACRYLIC: Moderately priced, acrylic rugs resist fading and crushing and are easy to clean (although they aren't as stain-resistant as wool or nylon). They also are soft to the touch and nonallergenic, perfect for family rooms and dining rooms.

• NYLON: Moderately priced, nylon rugs are the strongest synthetic fiber, standing up to stains, mildew, and abrasion very well. They are easy to clean and soft. But nylon rugs are static-prone, so keep them out of office areas with computers. Instead, place them in family rooms, dining rooms, kitchens, and bathrooms.

• POLYESTER: Less expensive than wool or nylon, polyester rugs are similar to wool in look, but much tougher. They are very durable and resistant to stains, as well as easy to clean. Plus, they are static-resistant, so they're ideal for home offices.

• OLEFIN: Moderately priced, olefin rugs are primarily indoor-outdoor rugs because they can withstand moisture and are very durable and easy to clean. Olefin rugs are also stain-resistant and static-resistant, so they're perfect for patios, kitchens, home offices, kids' bedrooms, and dining rooms.

5 If you can't find a large rug you like, pair two smaller ones for a big look.

6 Use a pad to protect floors, hold the rug in place, and cushion your feet.

7 Furniture should fit in the rug border, or the legs should overlap the edge.

chapter
FIVE

{ STORAGE & ORGANIZATION

- **CASE STUDY:** Clutter Control

- How to Organize Your Closet

- Order in the House

- Leave It at the Door

The Wrights chose furnishings for style and for kid safety. New windows, *below*, have blinds sandwiched between the glass, nixing a cord-choking hazard. The round coffee table, *below middle*, eliminates pointy corners. The new carpet, *bottom*, is wool sisal for hands-and-knees softness, cleanability, and durability.

safetyzone

Amazing storage space could be right under your nose in the middle of your living room. All you have to do is move your sofa to find it. Too often, living room furniture hugs the walls of the room, leaving a swath up the middle for foot traffic, scattered toys, or lingering laundry baskets. But by giving your sofa a tug and a twist into that hollow center, you can put the void to work, creating a secret storage spot and dividing the room into two purpose-driven areas.

That's the theory Thomas and Jeni Wright formed when they laid out the living room in the 1970s ranch they are gradually remodeling in Johnston, Iowa. With toddler Maya and her newborn sister, Piper (born a week after these photos were taken), the Wrights needed to make room for toys but didn't want them to take center stage.

"Before you have kids, you think you are going to have a playroom somewhere in the house and that the kids will be off playing in it. In reality, after you have kids, you learn that they want to be where you are and you want to keep an eye on them," Jeni says with an enlightened laugh. "We wanted to make this a living space for us and a play space for them. You see right into the living room from the entry, so we wanted it to look nice for people coming in the door. And we wanted space for a piano. We needed it to be three spaces instead of one," she says.

the sofa situation
The Wrights bought a dark leather sofa (durable for kids and pets) and angled it in the middle of the room to face the fireplace and the new, low media cabinet, *opposite top*, with gridded-veneer sliding doors. Behind the sofa hides the secret storage weapon: a sofa table that doubles as a toy organizer. Bins, lidded file boxes, and drawer cabinets keep toys, books, and trinkets in order, but if someone pops by while the kids are playing, the sofa screens much of the clutter.

To complete the conversation corner of the room, Jeni re-covered a pair of old tag-sale armchairs, *opposite bottom,* with a new cherry

SENSIBLE STORAGE

1 **SOFA SNEAKERY**
Face the sofa toward the entry, then camouflage clutter behind it.

2 **TUCK AND ROLL**
Stash chic boxes under the sofa table, and use wheeled toy crates for mobility.

storagezone

MAKE THIS WORK FOR YOU
Five more ways to use this idea

SPACE SMART

No toys to hide at your house? This sofa-angling tactic can camouflage more than kid clutter. Use the space to keep commonly used items within reach, yet out of plain sight. Is your sofa . . .

ALSO A SLEEPER? Place a trunk or three-drawer dresser behind the sofa to store extra bedding.
NEAR ELECTRONICS? Store movies and music in bins, boxes, or slotted holders under a sofa table.
BY THE DINING ROOM? Place a small dresser behind the sofa to hold linens and accessories.
WHERE YOU READ? Sneak two low bookshelves back there to align books and magazine holders.
WHERE YOU CRAFT? Sort knitting supplies, scrapbook embellishments, or snapshots in drawer bins or covered boxes under a tall table.

3 STOW AND GO
Don't fret over fancy toy sorters. Open bins catch clutter more quickly.

4 SORT IT ALL OUT
Having fewer toys out helps toddlers learn to pick up and sort easily.

5 DON'T BE SO CUTE
Leather or linen bins and jewelry drawers stow kid stuff in style.

6 WATCH LESS, PLAY MORE
Toddlers spend less time in a TV trance if cabinet doors are kept closed.

1 **OUTTA SIGHT**
Behind an angled sofa, define a play area that contains kid gear.

2 **ON TARGET**
A round red rug acts as a bull's-eye, drawing kids to the designated play zone.

wool upholstery fabric and chose a low, round cocktail table without sharp corners that Maya could hurt herself on. "It is table height for Maya when she sits on the floor," Jeni says. "She does try to turn it into a stage and dance floor, though."

The cabinet behind the chairs conceals a television and shallow shelves for books, videos, DVDs, and CDs. "We wanted to hide the television because kids aren't reminded to watch it if it is covered up, especially at Maya's age," Jeni says. "We also wanted to remove the risk of kids tipping over a television on a stand."

the play space

Between the sofa table and the back corner of the room is the designated play zone anchored by a round red rug, *below*. "Maya loves that rug! I think the big red circle in the middle of the space tells a 2-year-old that's a space for her," Jeni says. A pair of wooden toy bins on casters can scoot around as needed, and they make stuffed animals and dress-up clothes accessible so "that black hole thing doesn't happen like it does in a big toy box with a lid," she adds.

A baby grand piano may seem unusual in a children's play area, but not when your dad is a self-taught piano player who learned violin as a child and has sung in bands since high school. Having music a part of the girls' daily life is important to the Wrights. "Tom is so musical. He can just sit down at the piano and make up a song for the kids," Jeni says. "It's a stress reliever for him and a way to be creative and silly with the girls in a fun and relaxing way."

Who'd have thought this many good things could be achieved by simply moving the sofa to the center of a room?

play zone

By adding a piano to the play space, Maya enjoys music daily, crooning and keying with Dad, *top*. Wooden toy bins on casters, *above middle*, can roll around the room as wanted. They hold dress-up clothes that Abraham the hound dog often finds himself wearing, *above*.

3 THE KIDDIE TABLE
Skip the plastic. Wood tables and chairs look better in a living space.

4 JUST DREAM
Dress-up clothes spur creativity and create less clutter than bitsy toys.

5 COLOR CAMOUFLAGE
Using a primary hue in your living room decor helps toys blend in.

6 NUMBERS CONTROL
Too much toy clutter? Stow some out of sight, then rotate occasionally.

decorating for grown-ups

How do Thomas, Jeni, and Maya Wright, *left,* blend kid stuff into grown-up decor? Jeni says color and good furniture shapes are key. First, choose a primary color to ground your color scheme. "So many toys are in primary colors; having the red in here makes them not look so out of place," Jeni explains.

Second, choose children's furniture with sophisticated lines. Jeni bought the table and chairs, *opposite bottom,* because the style and red-stained finish look more like real furniture than typical sets. "It is important for kid furniture to be comfortable enough for adults to sit on, too—we do, and they are!"

MUSIC MAKER
Placing a piano by the play area makes music a part of daily life for the family.

CONVERSATION AREA
By facing the sofa and chairs in the front corner by the TV cabinet, adults can visit and keep eyes and ears on the kids at play.

SOFA SPECTACULAR
The success of this room all starts here—the sofa angled in the middle of the room divides the conversation and play areas while concealing powerful storage behind its back.

BULL'S-EYE!
A red circle rug marks the spot for play—behind the clutter-camouflaging sofa.

HOW TO ORGANIZE
your closet

What's a girl to do when she has tons of clothes but nowhere to put them? Organize her closet, of course! Here's how to claim every inch of space you have, no matter what size the closet.

bifold door

single door

walk-in

TIME TO TOSS
deciding what to keep and what to kick out

1 Does it fit?
At least once a year, or even once a season depending on how small your closet is, try on each item of clothing in front of a full-length mirror. Be honest with yourself. (After all, your organization is at stake!) Decide whether the style is a good fit for your current body type (not your "someday" body).

2 Do you wear it?
If you can't remember the last time you wore that oh-so-trendy peasant skirt or knit poncho (no matter how cute it was when you bought it), then it's probably time to donate it or sell it at a garage sale. A good rule of thumb: If you haven't worn the item in a year or more, it's safe to get rid of it.

3 Is it in good shape?
Threadbare and worn apparel isn't part of that boho chic trend; it looks messy. If items need a quick repair—a patched knee, a hemmed seam, a reattached button or zipper—set them in a pile for a tailor. If the item is ripped, badly stained, or full of holes, it's time to toss it in the trash or rip it up for dust rags.

STICK WITH IT
A pair of stick-on utility hooks helps squeeze every inch of space out of this slender wall. Easy to use and cheap, these hooks are deceptively strong and keep soft items from getting crushed.

SEASONAL STOWAWAY
When winter is done, bulky jackets and sweaters don't need to steal prime hanging or shelf space in your closet. Instead, stash them in a large cardboard box on the top shelf. Clean winter boots will fit nicely alongside, and when it's time to bundle up again, out-of-season summer clothes and sandals can take their place.

Hidden behind the hanging clothes on the back wall, this coat-hook rack doubles as a smart belt and scarf hanger in what was untapped closet storage space.

GOOD IDEA

LIVE LARGE
make the most of a small space

Even a small closet is packed with storage opportunities; it just requires you to be clever in finding them. For instance, in this single-door closet, a simple self-assembled shelving unit provides loads of adjustable space for folded t-shirts, jeans, and sweaters, while also accommodating boxes and baskets filled with camisoles and undergarments. An easy-to-install bar allows dress and work clothes to hang. Even the back of the door becomes a hanging shoe rack, with a few pockets devoted to small accessories.

BAUBLES AND DOODADS
A soft felt jewelry tray provides extra storage in narrow spaces. One side holds earrings, bracelets, and necklaces in scratch-resistant bowls, while the other holds a watch, ring, and loose change.

TO THE RACK
With pressed shirts, jackets, and dresses taking up most of the hanging space, this clever wall-mounted trouser rack fits snugly on the depth of the side wall and provides 10 spots to hang dress pants. Plus, the rods swivel, making it easy to grab just one pair of pants at a time.

GET HOOKED
Hidden inside the closet, a peel-and-stick plastic multihook mini rack provides belt storage without taking up shelf space. Plus, the hooks are fairly deep, holding more belts than might seem possible.

DYNAMIC DUO
sharing coveted space with your mate

Sharing a closet with your partner requires skillful planning and a diplomat's ability to divvy up space. Stackable, self-assembled storage units with adjustable cubbies and shelves provide structured places to store folded polos and jeans, plus several pairs of shoes. Canvas totes store exercise gear away from other clothes, while a high shelf installed overhead provides a spot to stash out-of-season attire in neat wicker baskets.

CLOSET ENVY
Whether you love or hate your closet probably depends on how organized it is. For a space worth falling head over heels for, consider these.

❶ closet system
Whether modest or grand, invest in a closet system to fit your space and budget. Ranging from custom solid wood to modular semi-custom particle board to coated wire, these systems have the components and accessories needed to transform any closet into a storage-savvy space.

❷ hang time
Double hanging rods are great—if they accommodate your clothes. Be sure to measure lengths before installing rods. Here's a general guide for clothing measurements:
pants folded: 20-23"
blazers/shirts/skirts: 36-42"
short dresses/pants hung by the cuff: 48-50"
long dresses/coats: 60-70"

❸ a step above
There's no one-size-fits-all when it comes to shoe storage. Standard shoe shelves, storage cubes, and boxes work wonders but may not accommodate all shoe sizes and heights. Be aware you may need to stow larger shoes sideways or stacked or find alternate storage for high heels and fashion boots.

❹ floor to ceiling
Though harder to reach, don't overlook (or underestimate) storage on the floor or near the ceiling. Low covered boxes tuck neatly on the floor under hanging clothes or stack several high on upper shelves and are perfect for stowing seasonal items or keepsakes not often accessed.

walk-in

RISE TO THE TOP

Large drawers pack lots of storage capacity, but they can get messy fast. Use drawer organizers to keep stacks from sliding. And place clothing strategically in drawers—the accessible top spot should be reserved for items worn daily.

HAVE ROOM TO ROAM

Walk-in closets get all the love because they have tons of room. But a large space with no organization is a recipe for daily stress. So count the clothing items in your closet and decide how many you want hung or folded, then create the system you need for the space you have.

PUT YOUR BEST FOOT FORWARD

A 4 × 5-foot mirror, cut at a local glass shop, transforms the back part of the walk-in-closet into a dressing room complete with a shoe bench to try on heels.

chic design that's functional

Removing one of the shelves opened up space to lean a small wall mirror (ideal for trying on jewelry) and display a few personal mementos. It's also the perfect spot to store perfume because your closet is a cool, dry place, and you can easily spritz it on while getting dressed.

KEEP IT CLEAN

A canvas tote filled with laundry supplies—stain remover, lint roller, static-cling reducer, and ironing starch—makes last-minute touch-ups easy and is ideally situated just above the laundry bin.

TIE ONE ON

Mounted on the side of the shelving unit behind the dress shirts, this sliding rack offers plenty of spots to store ties; it tucks out of view when not in use.

BE SHELF SMART

Perhaps the best part about a walk-in closet is its multifunctionality—it can hold everything! There's plenty of space for work and play attire, plus a three-bin laundry sorter, towels, pillows, linens, and storage for out-of-season garments.

packed with storage potential

Located in a spot where it's easy to grab things on the way out and drop them off on the way in, this shelf nook is the perfect catchall for pocket items. In the drawer, a long, removable canvas organizer keeps socks in one place.

The house is a mess, and you're in distress! But you can escape the chaos of clutter. Here's how to take control of four troublesome storage zones and reclaim your peace of mind.

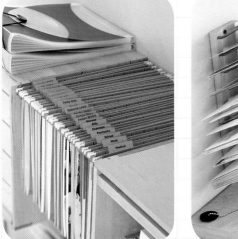

FILE RATHER THAN PILE
The "handle it once" rule keeps papers from piling up. Immediately toss, file, or pass on paperwork rather than revisiting it later. Labeled hanging files, *far left,* are one way to organize papers up and out of the way.

YOU'VE GOT MAIL
Organize mail, *left,* so it's processed daily, and consider responding via phone or e-mail when it's quicker than traditional post. A dedicated peg for receipts and a pen on a chain mean those items won't easily go missing.

A TIDY DESK
be willing to rework your space
Whether at home or in corporate cubicle land, an efficient, clutter-free office space, *opposite,* is essential to bringing a bit of sanity to your day. Let storage components climb the walls, and rearrange your space so regularly used supplies are accessible and others are out of the way.

OPEN-AND-SHUT CASE
Keep work surfaces tidy by stashing office supplies out of sight. Choose small-scale tape dispensers, staplers, and pencil sharpeners and such, *below left,* because full-size ones hog more space and don't often fit in drawers.

HANDY HELPERS
Stored by the batch and easy to snatch, clips, bands, and miscellaneous bits claim untapped territory. Spice jars, *below,* secured with commercial-grade hook-and-loop tape under cabinets do the trick.

Organizing your home isn't a one-shot effort. Once a space is tidy, you've got to keep it that way. But if you try to organize every space at once, it'll become a frustrating and unbearable chore. Instead, set aside manageable bites of time each week to tackle a trouble spot or reassess an orderly one.

SMART SORTER
Put an end to a jumble of a jewelry with a ceramic egg tray, *above*, found in the kitchen supply aisle. Tuck earrings and necklaces away in little nests, never to be lost or separated again.

OUT WITH IT
Your back will appreciate bins that pull out from under cabinets, making contents easy to find and reach. Determine whether your cabinet will accept a side-mount track, *above*, or one that mounts at the bottom.

ALL STRAPPED IN
Taking a cue from luggage that secures contents in elastic pouches, we used fabric glue to affix different lengths of elastic bands inside an undercounter canvas basket, *above*. They'll keep bottles from tumbling.

THE MORNING RUSH
essentials that are ready when you are

If it will function better, don't hesitate to alter a perfectly good vanity cabinet. We replaced doors with swing rods, *above*, that hold hand towels on one arm and a privacy curtain on the other. Secured to the cabinet side are a hair dryer holster and hooks for a hairbrush and mirror. If there's no room to tuck everything away, never fear. Display pretty soaps, nail polish, and jewelry in a tray.

IN CONTROL

There's a remote control for everything these days, but what good are they when misplaced? Stop searching and identify a place like our space-savvy bin, *above,* mounted inside the cabinet door.

ANYBODY'S GAME

Establishing a dedicated game drawer means you'll know just where to find dice and a deck of cards when you need them. A divided bin, *above,* is a winning solution for corralling all those tiny game pieces.

FAMILY FUN TIME
containing the media frenzy

From movies to music to magazines, today's mayhem of media gear demands a place to call home. With adjustable shelves and generous drawer space, this versatile cabinet, *above,* stores a multitude of electronic toys as well as reading material, photo albums (yes, print and organize those digital pictures), and games.

laundry

GOT YOU PEGGED
Replacing door panels with pegboard, *above*, creates storage on both sides of the door (perfect for our stain removal chart). Staples at hardware stores, the board and hanging accessories are also popping up in decorating catalogs.

FORGOTTEN TREASURES
It's good practice to check pockets before laundering clothes. You avoid damage that coins or crayons might do to the washer, dryer, or garments, and you just might find a tasty treat or modest tip for your hard work. A labeled container such as this jar, *above*, helps assure pocket dwellers get back to their rightful owners.

TIME TO TOSS
deciding what to keep and what to kick out

❶ Is it expired?
If past its prime, it's to-go time. Milk and meds aren't the only things with expiration dates these days. Printer ink cartridges, suntan lotion, toothpaste—if it's beyond its expiration date, it isn't likely to function at its best.

❷ Is it used?
Use it or lose it. This may seem like a no-brainer, but how many partial bottles of you-name-it have lurked unused in your cabinet for years? Whether it's chartreuse nail polish or a box of cassette tapes collecting dust, give it the boot.

❸ Is it a duplicate?
No need for multiples. Do you really need two ironing boards? Three phone books? Fifty old towels-turned-rags? Enough said.

❹ Is it a fit?
Would you buy it today? If you didn't already own the item, ask yourself whether you'd buy it now. Maybe your taste in music has changed or the size and color of that vase doesn't fit your rearranged room. Edit out those oddities.

Leave keg-size containers at the store and opt for smaller bottles of ultraconcentrated formulas that take up far less space and clean just as well. Be sure to read directions so you use the right amount.

SPACE SMART

GOOD, CLEAN FUN
breezy ways to wash away clutter

Sorting laundry by color with help from a multibag hamper helps wash day go faster. The flip top on this one, *opposite*, even serves as a folding table or, with a pad, functions as an ironing board. Housing an iron and a clothes rod on the side of the cabinet takes advantage of underutilized space. This rod folds down when not in use, but you might consider a retractable clothesline for its hardworking, space-saving qualities.

E100S 47 KODAK E100S

THINK INSIDE THE BOX
On Brice's living room
storage wall, large boxes
stow files; small ones tidy
office supplies and camera
equipment. Accessories
add life, while voids on the
shelves let the eye rest.

6

Blank canvas Organization just feels better when you put a label on the carton, doesn't it? You'll always know where to find your thingamajigs (or your sweaters or shoes) with these foldable canvas boxes.

It works for her Perfectly sized to fit on a 12-inch-deep shelf, these pandan boxes are the saving grace for homeowner Brice Gaillard's paperwork and office supplies. Woven of pandan leaf, the boxes come in several hues, and the sturdy lids allow for stacking one atop another or are shallow enough to tuck under the bed.

Basket case A touch global stripe, a bit boho breeze, these Mandan storage boxes are a free-spirited way to stash your stuff (files and photos—or the swishy skirts and the espadrilles you've sadly put away for fall). Lids keep items from collecting dust.

Press box If you don't have storage boxes for your magazines, you should. By slipping stacks of publications into these faux leather sorters, you'll reclaim space on your tables (and floors, counters, etc.) you forgot you had. Many boxes like these even accomodate hanging file folders!

Whatcha bin thinking? The icons on these powder-coated steel Muck bins give you a tongue-in-cheek clue to what small items you can hide inside—hand tools, sports gear, or pet toys and treats—then stash on a shelf. They even attract magnets in case you want to post a note or label.

store it

With a new bookcase and a clever new desk with file boxes, Brice keeps her working papers (everything from billing sheets, *top*, to home design books and magazines, *below*) close at hand, yet stylishly displayed.

HEAD FOR THE HORIZON
Play a trick on your eyes. Stare at the painting in the dinette. Feel like you're flying? That's because the painting has a definite horizon line. "By hanging a piece like this on a blank wall you give the illusion of depth to a room," Brown explains. "This visual trick leads the eye beyond the wall. A beautiful landscape accomplishes this best."

color it in
The living room's orange and blue accent colors carry into the kitchen as a way to link the two rooms.

stay slim
In the small dinette, armless bamboo chairs are less bulky. These were bought unfinished online and painted brilliant blue.

No room for furniture? Windows long and in the way of wall art? Go low with scootable ottomans that seat and store.

By hanging window curtains and bookcase curtains on the ceiling, the room looks taller (and brick walls here weren't dinged).

✳ start with a plan

Always start a design project by sketching a floor plan, designer Kenneth Brown advises. "Walls are the only boundary—what lies between is a blank canvas," he says. "It can also give you a fresh perspective of the room. You'll be amazed at the potential you see from this bird's-eye view." You'll see that walls can actually be powerful tools. **1.** Shallow wall shelves not only serve as a photo gallery; they're also spots to drop keys and sunglasses inside the door. Plus, they visually extend the walls. **2.** Curtains give two bookshelves colorful flair; the mirror between them reflects sunlight, making the room brighter. **3.** A small side chair along a sliver of wall provides lounging space without taking up depth. **4.** A tall cabinet puts the TV up high and stores drinks down low.

$400
room divider
That's the
approximate cost of
materials; a buddy
helped make it.

$800
sofa savvy
Saw it, bought it,
took it home
that day.

the five-day decorator

Are you letting the decorating process slow you down? Why make it hard? This couple furnished a condo in no time flat. Here's how.

$1,200
tv chest
A splurge at a local antiques store, the Japanese chest adds history.

smalltalk

Add artsy accessories that spark curiosity and conversation. A huge bowl on the coffee table, *top* and *middle*, holds game pieces for spontaneous play and a textural look. Vellum paper wraps give books an ethereal quality, *bottom*.

To say that King and Ann Au kept a tight schedule when decorating their San Francisco condo is an understatement. With work as a photographer taking King to the City by the Bay more frequently, this Des Moines couple decided to stop paying steep hotel rates and invest in a condo in this prime real-estate market. Plus, it would be a great place to spend school breaks and vacations with sons Sam, 10, and Simon, 6.

With the deal closed, King started decorating. Knowing that he and Ann wanted a neutral, modern aesthetic—and unwilling to wait in empty rooms for custom orders—he went shopping and got the rooms up to snuff in just five days.

How did he do it? King had a great starting point. He and Ann, a jewelry designer, had already purchased a metal horse sculpture at a San Francisco art show. "We bought it before we even found the condo," he admits. "We always like to have a little sculpture—not all flat, two-dimensional pieces. It clicked volumetrically. We liked the shapes and form."

He liked the idea of using the sculpture to divide the long living space that comprises kitchen, dining, and sitting areas. But the sculpture wouldn't have enough visual mass to do the trick alone. "The space sort of roamed. I needed a screen to give each area a sense of space and function," King says. He first looked in stores but couldn't find a screen tall enough to be effective yet narrow enough to walk around. Luckily, a buddy helped him make one quickly out of 1 × 6s, screws, black spray paint, and superstrong polycarbonate plastic sheets.

Time to shop. With the room divided and a rough sketch of a floor plan with needed pieces, King hit a handful of favorite retail stores, boutiques, and antiques shops. "I did cash-and-carry," he says of every purchase. In five days he jetted through a lot of stores, but in the end, purchases came from just five. **STORE NO. 1** netted a gray-blue sofa that could back the screen and anchor the sitting area, plus a matching chair—and a wonderful geometric square-pattern rug to underscore it all. At **STORE NO. 2**, he found a great coffee table, but the rectangle was too small. Rather than hunt further, he bought two and set up a square. The matching side table is from a trio of nesting tables—the other two are used elsewhere in the home. At the same store, a framed set of black-and-white tulip photos caught his photographer's eye, and he added it to the cart. **STORE NO. 3** was a local antiques shop where a Japanese chest looked like the perfect piece to use as an entertainment center. The $1,200 price tag was more reasonable than many of the new pieces he'd seen. Plus, it could be used in different ways and rooms in the future. The dining table and chairs were the last pieces to be found. "I wanted to find the personality I liked, but most tables were too big,"

SWIFT THINKING

1 **PLAY FAVORITES**
Go straight to stores you know stock your look. When time is tight, you can't go custom. Be time-wise. Shop boutiques by day, retail chains by night.

2 **PICK A PALETTE**
Focus on furniture and accents in just three general tones so items from different stores blend easily and quickly. Here? Blues, browns, and reds.

$50
framed art
Spotted the black-and-white photos at IKEA.

$80/two
coffee tables
One was too small; a pair gives more volume.

$450
area rug
Adds graphic pattern underfoot.

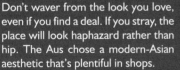

3 **STICK TO A STYLE**
Don't waver from the look you love, even if you find a deal. If you stray, the place will look haphazard rather than hip. The Aus chose a modern-Asian aesthetic that's plentiful in shops.

4 **DON'T FORGET THE ART**
Hanging wall art and adding sculpture immediately make a place feel as if you've lived there for years. Pieces don't have to be expensive; the walls just can't all be empty!

5 **OH, GO AHEAD AND MATCH**
Even though eclecticism is in, if you're in a hurry, it's OK for a sofa and chair or set of accent tables to match. Get your key pieces in place and find other ways to be eclectic later.

1 **VISIT FAIRS**
Local art shows and fairs are great sources for wall art and sculpture at a good value. (C'mon, get beyond the poster prints of the 1980s!)

2 **ASK THE PROF**
King Au suggests searching galleries in college towns for professors' work. He found a small sculpture done by a Berkeley prof in the 1960s.

King says. He found the answer in a discount mass merchant, **STORE NO. 4.** "I liked the richness and texture of the top, but the leg style didn't fit, so I chopped off the legs and apron and put on metal legs," he says. In all of his savvy shopping, King also wanted to patronize a local, independent boutique with unique offerings—he did that at **STORE NO. 5,** splurging on teak-and-buffalo-hide dining chairs. (Remember, the table was a bargain!)

Include the art

As artists themselves, King and Ann believe good art can come from many sources. The sculpture by the TV is from a gallery, and the horse sculpture came from an art show. But the photography above the TV is from IKEA. "I look for the visual content, not the name association," King says. Even kitchen shelving serves as a gallery for vintage signage lettering, and the kitchen wall has a framed corkboard where the family collect postcards that catch their eye.

The true time test? King had everything in place to host a baby shower on day six—and the space accommodated it beautifully.

big ideas

$2–$25
letter-perfect
Say something with vintage sign letters from various sources.

The Aus' large-scale art ideas are both fun and fine. A framed corkboard, *top*, holds a postcard collection that Sam and Simon, *above middle*, enjoy expanding. The horse sculpture, *bottom*, was the first piece the couple bought for the condo.

3 **INEXPENSIVE IS OK**
Names don't necessarily matter to King. He's not afraid to mix pricey pieces with inexpensive ones. He responds to imagery rather than to price or fame.

4 **MAKE IT YOURSELF**
Fill big, empty walls with your own art on the cheap. The Aus tack artsy postcards on a huge framed corkboard and use letters to spell clever phrases on the kitchen's open shelving.

5 **SO SNAP-HAPPY**
Photography is often an affordable art medium. Or supersize your own digital snapshots in color or convert them to black-and-white and then print to canvas to avoid the cost of pricey frames.

$400/ea.
chic chairs
A splurge, but couldn't resist 'em at a local shop.

$450
dining table
Put on new metal legs.

TABLE TALK
A dining table on wheels ensures ultimate flexibility for a change of arrangement.

ISLAND ESCAPE
An existing island delineates the kitchen and serves as a handy serving buffet or bar.

PATIO POWER
Floor-to-ceiling glass doors let the patio serve as an extended area of the living room.

GREAT POSITIONING
Backing the sofa against the screen defines the sitting and dining areas yet still allows sunlight throughout the space.

resources

These are some of our favorite sources for finding real-life décor.

ANTHROPOLOGIE; 800/309-2500; anthropologie.com.

ART.COM; 800/952-5592; art.com.

BALLARD DESIGNS; 800/367-2775; ballarddesigns.com (product line varies).

BASSETT FURNITURE INDUSTRIES, INC.; 276/629-6000; bassettfurniture.com.

BED BATH & BEYOND; 800/462-3966; bedbathandbeyond. com (product line varies).

BEHR PREMIUM PLUS PAINTS; 800/854-0133, ext. 2; behr.com. Sold exclusively at Home Depot USA; homedepot.com.

BELLACOR; 877/723-5522; bellacor.com.

BENJAMIN MOORE; 888/236-6667; benjaminmoore.com.

BLISSLIVING HOME; 866/952-5477; blisslivinghome.com.

BLOOMINGDALE'S; 800/555-7467; bloomingdales.com.

BROCADE HOME; 800/276-2233; brocadehome.com.

BROYHILL FURNITURE INDUSTRIES, INC.; broyhillfurniture.com.

CALICO CORNERS; 800/213-6366; calicocorners.com.

CB2; 800/606-6252; cb2.com.

CHIASSO; 800/654-3570; chiasso.com.

COMPANY C, INC.; 800/818-8288; companyc.com.

THE COMPANY STORE; 800/285-3696; thecompanystore.com (product line varies).

THE CONTAINER STORE; 800/786-7315; containerstore.com.

COSTCO; 800/774-2678; costco.com.

CRATE & BARREL; 800/967-6696; crateandbarrel.com (product line varies).

DASH AND ALBERT; 800/557-2035; dashandalbert.com.

DREXEL HERITAGE FURNISHINGS, INC.; drexelheritage.com.

DUTCH BOY PAINTS; 800/828-5669; dutchboy.com.

ETSY; etsy.com; e-mail: support@etsy.com.

ETHAN ALLEN HOME INTERIORS; 888/324-3571; ethanallen.com.

FLOR; 866/281-3567; flor.com.

GARNET HILL; 800/622-6216; garnethill.com (product line varies).

HANCOCK FABRICS, INC.; 877/322-7427; hancockfabrics.com.

HOME DECORATOR'S COLLECTION; 800/245-2217; homedecorators.com.

THE HOME DEPOT USA, INC.; homedepot.com.

HORCHOW HOME CATALOG; 800/456-7000; horchow.com.

IKEA; in the United States: 877/345-4532; in Canada: 888/932-4532; ikea.com.

JCPENNEY HOME COLLECTION; 800/222-6161; jcpenney.com.

JO-ANN STORES; 888/739-4120; jo-annstores.com.

KMART; 800/866-0086; kmart.com.

LAMPS PLUS; 800/782-1967; lampsplus.com.

LA-Z-BOY; lazboy.com.

LOWE'S; 800/445-6937; lowes.com.

MACY'S; 800/289-6229; macys.com.

MARSHALLS; 800/627-7425; marshallsonline.com (product line varies).

MITCHELL GOLD + BOB WILLIAMS; 800/789-5401; mgandbw.com.

MOMA DESIGN STORE, 800/447-6662; momastore.org.

NATIONAL GUILD OF PROFESSIONAL PAPERHANGERS, INC.; 800/254-6477; ngpp.org.

ORGANIZE.COM; 800/600-9817; organize.com.

PIER 1 IMPORTS; 800/245-4595; pier1.com.

POTTERY BARN; 800/922-5507; potterybarn.com (product line varies).

RESTORATION HARDWARE; 800/910-9836; restorationhardware.com.

ROOM & BOARD; 800/486-6554; roomandboard.com.

ROSANNA, INC.; 877/343-3779; rosannainc.com.

THE SHERWIN-WILLIAMS CO.; 800/474-3794; sherwin-williams.com.

TARGET STORES; 800/800-8800 for a retail store near you; target.com (product line varies).

THOMAS PAUL; thomaspaul.com.

THOMASVILLE FURNITURE INDUSTRIES, INC.; 800/225-0265; thomasville.com.

T.J. MAXX; 800/285-6299; tjmaxx.com (product line varies).

URBAN OUTFITTERS; 800/282-2200; urbanoutfitters.com.

VIVA TERRA; 800/233-6011; vivaterra.com.

WAL-MART; 800/925-6278; walmart.com (product line varies).

WAVERLY; waverly.com (product line varies).

WEST ELM; 866/428-6468; westelm.com (product line varies).

WISTERIA; 800/767-5490; wisteria.com.

WORLD MARKET; 877/967-5362; worldmarket.com.

Z-GALLERIE; 800/908-6748; zgallerie.com.

index